Rout

CASTE

A Comparative Study

CASTE

A Comparative Study

by
A. M. HOCART

Routledge
Taylor & Francis Group

First published in 1950 by Methuen & Co. Ltd.

This edition first published in 2018 by Routledge
2 Park Square, Milton Park, Abingdon, Oxon, OX14 4RN
and by Routledge
711 Third Avenue, New York, NY 10017

Routledge is an imprint of the Taylor & Francis Group, an informa business

© 1950 Taylor & Francis

Publisher's Note
The publisher has gone to great lengths to ensure the quality of this reprint but
points out that some imperfections in the original copies may be apparent.

Disclaimer
The publisher has made every effort to trace copyright holders and welcomes
correspondence from those they have been unable to contact.
A Library of Congress record exists under ISBN: 51003509

ISBN 13: 978-1-138-55596-9 (hbk)
ISBN 13: 978-1-138-56492-3 (pbk)
ISBN 13: 978-1-315-12269-4 (ebk)

CASTE

A Comparative Study

by

A. M. HOCART

METHUEN & CO. LTD. LONDON
36 Essex Street, Strand, W.C.2

First published in 1950

CATALOGUE NO. 5275/U

PRINTED IN GREAT BRITAIN

Foreword

ARTHUR MAURICE HOCART was born in Guernsey in 1884, and was educated there, at Brussels, and at Oxford, where he was a Classical and Senior Scholar of Exeter College. After studying psychology at the University of Berlin, he went to the South Pacific, where he conducted anthropological researches, some of them in collaboration with Dr. W. H. R. Rivers, in Fiji, Tonga, Samoa, and elsewhere. He was also for some time Headmaster of the native school at Lau, Fiji. His researches produced many learned articles and a book on the *Lau Islands*. After war service in France, he was appointed Archæological Commissioner in Ceylon, and during the ten years that he held this post conducted important excavations and wrote many articles on the history and archæology of Ceylon and the customs and beliefs of the Sinhalese. In 1934 he was appointed Professor of Sociology in the University of Cairo. In this capacity he gained the friendship of many of his students, and visited many parts of Egypt. He died, after a short illness, in 1939, leaving a widow who had helped him in much of his later work.

While in Fiji he had made a thorough study of the native religion and social organization, and found that they were but two aspects of the same thing. When he made a similar study in Ceylon, he found not only that the same principle applied there, but also that, in spite of the much higher degree of civilization which the Sinhalese had reached, the significant patterns which occurred were very similar to those of Fiji. Turning to the relevant literature on other peoples, he found, wherever the information was adequate, that the same patterns reappeared

almost everywhere. In his book, *Kingship*, published while
he was in Ceylon, he showed that in whatever part of the
world kings are crowned or chiefs installed, the same
twenty-six features, or most of them, make up the ceremony. He also showed that initiation rites and marriage
ceremonies, wherever they occur, are modified versions
of the royal ritual.

In *Kings and Councillors*, published in Cairo, he showed
that priests, nobles, and officials, wherever found, originally owed their position to the parts which they played
in a ritual of which the king was the head.

Finally, in the present work, the last to be completed
before his death, he shows that it was not only kings,
priests and nobles who took part in the rites, but all
members of the community, and that for this purpose
they were organized in hereditary groups. Such groups
either still exist, or have left traces, in many parts of the
world, but it is only in India that they are known as
"castes."

Hocart's theory in essence is, then, that all human
communities were originally bodies of persons organized
for ritual purposes. These were various, but the chief
purpose was to secure "life." This does not necessarily
mean everlasting life, or even life after death, but a full
life—that is to say, a long life free from sickness, with
a sufficiency of whatever is considered necessary or desir-
able, including offspring. It is still believed by many that
this can be ensured by due performance of the rites.
Whether these rites be termed "magical" or "religious"
is largely a question of terminology; Hocart disapproved
of Frazer's attempt to draw a hard and fast line between
them.

At the head of the rites, from very early times, stood
the divine king. His principal duty was to be just—that
is to say, to see that all, whether gods or men, received

their due. If this were done, the rites would be performed correctly and without disturbance, and the rain would fall in due season. Since the divine king was god as well as man, the whole of his service was a ritual service, and his cook, barber, drummer, etc., were sacred persons, and the families which furnished them (the "castes") received, as a reward for their services to the king, and through him to the community as a whole, lands and other privileges. This does not mean that all members of the cook caste were always cooks. Hocart shows that this is not so in India, and, so far as is known, has never been so anywhere. The king's cook, in fact, need not actually cook at all, but merely supervise the preparation of the king's food. In England there is a family which used to provide the King's Champion at his coronation, but it did not consist of professional duellists.

The caste system, then, is a system for distributing throughout the community the various duties connected with the royal ritual and the king's service, which are largely the same, and for ensuring that these duties are performed only by those properly qualified to perform them—qualified, that is to say, both by heredity and knowledge of the rites. Most of the evidence for this comes, of course, from India and Ceylon, where the caste system has survived in a far more perfect form than elsewhere, but Hocart shows that comparable forms still exist in Polynesia and Melanesia, and that clear traces of them can be seen in ancient Greece and Rome, and in modern Egypt.

Hocart's theory seems in its main features incontrovertible, yet it has not been widely accepted. This is because it is at present fashionable to rationalize all customs, and to write up the "economic man" to the exclusion of that far older and more widespread type, the religious man, who, though he tilled and built and reared a family, believed that he could do these things successfully only so long as he played his allotted part in the ritual activities of his community.

It is, however, pretty safe to prophesy that the time will come when Hocart will be regarded as a pioneer of scientific sociology, and this book as one of his most important contributions to it.

RAGLAN

Preface

THE physicist can measure the shift of a spectral line in micromillimetres, and no one questions the value of his work. An implicit faith is abroad that his smallest measurements lead up to great things. The student of culture commands no such confidence. If he observes the shift of an accent, he is censured for wasting brain and time on unworthy minutiæ. If he attempts something on a grand scale his theories are dismissed as flights of imagination with no firm basis. He is caught in a vicious circle and vicious circles are most difficult to escape from. Yet the physicist escaped by plodding away in faith, patiently adding brick to brick, until at last even the blindest could see the edifice emerging.

There is no reason why the study of culture should not eventually arrive at the same point, perhaps not in the student's time, but thanks to his efforts. But he has to begin at the beginning, sorting out the excessive mass of material and reducing it to some order out of which the main lines begin to appear. Our generation is, as a matter of fact, beginning to formulate simple ideas that fit a large number of facts which formerly seemed unrelated. I shall instance more particularly the finding of recurrent structures or patterns in rituals and in myths.[1]

In my *Kings and Councillors* I looked for similar uniformities in social organization. Since the subject has been much neglected in favour of magic, numerous gaps

[1] See *Myth and Ritual* (London, 1933) and *The Labyrinth* (London, 1935), both ed. by S. H. Hooke. H. G. Quaritch Wales, *Siamese State Ceremonies* (London, 1931). Lord Raglan, *The Hero* (London, 1936). E. O. James, *Christian Myth and Ritual* (London, 1933).

were inevitable; but the aim was as much to point out the gaps to fill as those that had been filled. It was an attempt to show how small things might lead up to big things; but in order to do so the smallest had to be omitted lest they bewilder the reader. It was necessary to cut down the evidence to the bare minimum so that the general ideas might stand out. The object of the present work is to exhibit those smallest things out of which the biggest were constructed, to deal minutely with the arrangement of citizens into classes, so that the general ideas might be seen working themselves out in their minutest consequences. Depth could only be gained at the expense of breadth. What there occupied little more than a dozen pages is here expanded to a book, but the area and the scope have been reduced. There I embraced the world and society; here I have confined myself geographically to southern Asia and its extensions east and west, elementally to caste. Within these boundaries I have added a few societies which had been omitted in the sketch because they would have blurred the picture with too much detail.

The reader will do well to get a bird's-eye view from *Kings and Councillors* before plunging into the forest.

Something will have been achieved if the reader can be persuaded that the Indian caste system is not the isolated phenomenon it is often thought to be, but a species of a very widespread genus. Not being an isolated phenomenon, it cannot be understood in isolation; it will merely be misunderstood. More than once it will be shown in these pages how localized specialism leads away from the truth and comparative study returns to it. Comparison also saves time by cutting the tangled knots which controversy ties round texts.

In the handling of those texts I hope I have not brought

too much discredit on my teachers, the late Dr. L. R. Farnell and Professor A. A. MacDonell.

Sections I to V of the chapter on India are reproduced from Vol. IV of *Acta Orientalia* by kind permission of the Editor.

Contents

Abbreviations and Bibliography

Abbreviation	Explanation
Ait. Br.	*Aitareya Brāhmaṇa*, ed. Th. Aufrecht, Bonn, 1879. Trsl. A. B. Keith in *Rigveda Brahmanas*, Harvard Oriental Series, Cambridge, Mass., 1920.
Ar., *Pol.*	The *Politics* of Aristotle. The first figure is that of Bekker's ed., the second of Tauchnitz's.
A.S.C.	Archæological Survey of Ceylon.
A.S.I.	Archæological Survey of India.
Ath. Pol.	*Athenaiōn Politeia* attributed to Aristotle.
Br.	*Brāhmaṇa.*
C.J. Sc., *G.*	*Ceylon Journal of Science*, section G, London, Dulau and Co., Old Bond Street.
Digha.	*Dīgha nikāya* in the *Suttapiṭaka*, Pali Text Society, Oxford, 1890.
Dion. Hal.	Dionysius of Halikarnassus.
D'Oyly.	Sir John D'Oyly, *A Sketch of the Constitution of the Kandyan Kingdom*, Colombo, Government Printer, 1929.
Ep. Z.	*Epigraphia Zeylanica*, issued by the A.S.C., Clarendon Press, Oxford.
Gilbert.	G. Gilbert, *Griechische Staatsaltertümer*, Leipzig, 1881.
Hdt.	Herodotos.

Abbreviation	*Explanation*
Il.	*Iliad.*
Jataka.	(Buddhist Birth Stories), ed. V. Fausböll, London, 1877-97. Trsl. ed. Cowell, London, 1875, etc.
J.R.A.I.	*Journal of the Royal Anthropological Institute*, London.
Kings and Councillors.	By A. M. Hocart, Cairo, 1936 (also at Luzac and Co., 46 Great Russell Street, London, W.C.1).
Kingship.	By A. M. Hocart, Oxford, 1927.
Knox.	Robert Knox, *An Historical Relation of Ceylon*, reprint of 1911, London. The pages refer to the original edition as shown in the margin of the reprint.
Lau.	A. M. Hocart, *The Lau Islands*, Bishop Pauahi Museum, Honolulu, 1929.
MacDonell and Keith.	A. A. MacDonell and A. B. Keith, *Vedic Index of Names and Places*, London, 1912.
Maitr. Samh.	*Maitraiyanī Saṁhitā.*
Manu.	*Mānava Dharmaśāstra* or *Laws of Manu.*
Mem.	*Memoirs.*
Mhbh.	*Mahābhārata.*
Mhvs.	*Mahāvaṁsa*, including the *Cūlavaṁsa*, ed. and trsl. W. Geiger for the Pali Text Society, Oxford.
Muir.	J. Muir, *Original Sanskrit Texts.* five vols., 2nd ed., London, 1868-74.

Abbreviation	*Explanation*
Mysore Tribes and Castes, The	ed. Anantha Krishna Iyer, Mysore, 1930.
Nala.	*The Episode of Nala* from the *Mhbh.*, ed. Julius Eggeling, Edin. and London, 1913.
Od.	*Odyssey.*
Pauly-Wissowa.	*Real-lexikon der classischen Altertumswissenschaft*, Stuttgart, 1893, etc.
Progress of Man, The.	By A. M. Hocart, London, 1933.
Rep.	*Report.*
Sat. Br.	*Satapatha Brahmana*, Vol. II, of *White Yajur-Veda*, ed. A. Weber, 1849-59. Trsl. Julius Eggeling in *S.B.E.*
S.B.E.	*Sacred Books of the East*, ed. Max Muller, Oxford, 1882, etc.
Skt.	Sanskrit.
Temple of the Tooth.	A. M. Hocart, *The Temple of the Tooth in Kandy, Mem. A.S.C., IV*, London, 1931.
Thurston.	*Castes and Tribes of Southern India*, ed. Edgar Thurston, 7 vols., Madras, 1901 etc.
Trsl.	Translation; translated by.

Transliteration

c	.	.	.	like *ch* in English, Skt., Sinhalese, Rotuman.
ḍ	.	.	.	cerebral *d*, Skt.
ꭓ	.	.	.	like *th* in *then*, Fijian.
ṅ	.	.	.	like *ng* in sing. Skt., Tamil, Fijian, Tongan, Samoan, Rotuman.
ṇ	.	.	.	cerebral *n*, Skt., Tamil.
q	.	.	.	guttural *k*, Arabic.
ś	.	.	.	palatal *s*, Skt.
ṣ	.	.	.	like *sh* in English, Skt.
ṭ	.	.	.	cerebral *t*, Skt.

India

I

SO much has been written about caste without bringing about a decision in favour of any particular theory that the public is perhaps a little weary of the discussion. Yet the late M. Senart's admirable reasoning[1] has shown that definite progress can be made. He has, I think, achieved a positive result in disposing of two theories, the occupational and the racial, which are derived rather from preconceived notions about primitive society than from the facts they profess to explain, and least of all from the point of view of the people who have developed the system and work it at the present day, and who are therefore our best guides. The occupational theory, for instance, seizing upon the obvious fact that caste and profession or trade are closely connected, hastily concludes that caste is based solely on a man's occupation, and is the inevitable result of specialization in arts and crafts. If it had gone a little deeper it would have found that caste and craft are by no means as identical as is commonly supposed in Europe. Since this idea that an Indian is predestined to his craft by heredity is one of the main obstacles in the way of understanding the caste system we may be excused for dwelling on this point even after M. Senart's cogent little treatise.

It is not the case that an Indian has no choice of occupation, but must follow that of his father, shave or cook or fish, as his father did. I have had to explain to tourists labouring under that misconception that my

---

[1] *Les Castes dans l'Inde*, Ernest Leroux, 1896.

coolie gang, for instance, included anything from farmers, who probably had never handled a plough or sown a seed, down to drummers who may not know one end of the drum from the other, and cobblers who had never stitched a shoe; that the bar and commerce of Ceylon are largely in the hands of fishermen who would scorn to fish; that my food has been cooked by a farmer, by one who styles himself a merchant, but never, to my knowledge, by a member of the cook caste. Not all washermen wash, nor because you see a person washing are you safe in concluding that he is a washerman by caste. The state of affairs in Ceylon is this: a man may wash his own clothes; the mother, the elder sister, any one in the family can wash the clothes, "but," says my informant, "we do not take outside washing; it would be a disgrace to the caste." If clothes are given out to be washed, as is usual, they will be given to a washerman, if one is available; otherwise to a man of some other low caste. Not every man who drums is a drummer: in Ceylon you can often see women of good caste sitting round a big drum,[1] and whiling away the idleness of a festive day with varying rhythms; but neither their sex nor their caste would officiate as public drummers at a temple, a wedding, or a funeral. Farming is the vocation of the highest caste in Ceylon, yet washermen so habitually till the fields that they have special field superintendents who are distinguished by a different title from the field superintendents of the farmer folk.[2] This latitude is not modern, not brought about by the disturbing influence of European example, for Manu allows the priestly caste to live by agriculture and trade, a permission of which Brahmans in South India avail themselves.[3] The royal state was the prerogative of the

[1] *Rabāna.*

[2] *Vel pedi* as against *vel vidāne.*

[3] *Manu*, IV, 2 *ff.*; Thurston, *op. cit.*, I, 344.

royal or noble caste;[1] yet in ancient days low caste men, washermen and others, not uncommonly became kings.[2]

Evidently the common European notion that caste is hereditary handicraft does not tally with the facts. We must conclude that it derives from some other principle. We must search for that principle not in our minds, but in the minds of those people who practise the caste system, who have daily experience of it, and are thus most likely to have a feeling for what is essential in it.

If I go to seek for it among the Sinhalese and the Ceylon Tamils, it is for the simple reason that it is the only part of the Indian world where I have experience of caste as a living organism. Apart from that, it is not a bad area to seek in; for Ceylon, in spite of its roads, estates, Colombo, and a swarm of officials, still remains very archaic in some respects. One still gets some of the atmosphere of the Jatakas, that is of a very ancient India, long before the advent of Mohammedanism. The sequel will demonstrate this to some extent.

II

Before we can ask the people themselves with any hope of understanding them what is their idea of caste, we must have some acquaintance with the facts of the system, for they will inevitably assume some such knowledge, and if we have not got it we shall be talking at cross purposes. I will therefore give a very brief outline of the hierarchy as it exists in Ceylon.

The first caste among the Sinhalese was once the royal one, but it is now extinct. The former existence of the

[1] Usually described by Europeans as the warrior caste; but fighting, as we shall see, is only a derivative; the essence of their function is sovereignty, kingship, hence the names by which they are known in India.

[2] *Manu*, IV, 61; *Indian Art and Letters*, I, 19.

brahmanic or priestly caste is attested by ancient writings and by such place names as "brahman village". The disappearance of these two castes leaves the first rank to the farmers. They must once have shared equal honours with the merchants, a caste the former existence of which can be inferred from village names and the names of ancient streets.[1] Curiously enough this farmer aristocracy forms the vast majority of the population of the old Kandyan kingdom. On the coast their predominance is much reduced by the presence in great force of fishermen.

The members of the three leading castes, extinct or surviving, are known as the "good people." They are opposed to the "low castes," who comprise fishermen, smiths, washermen to the "good people," tailors, potters, weavers, cooks, lime-burners, grass-cutters, drummers, charcoal burners, washermen to the low castes, mat-makers, and, most despised of all, the Rodiyas, shunned by everyone.[2] These castes are again often subdivided: there are different ranks of farmers, and the fishermen are divided according as they fish with nets, rods, boats, and so on; the *vahuṇpura* and the *durava* are said to be an upper and a lower division of the same caste.

The Tamils of the North of Ceylon have much the same castes: the kings are extinct, the brahmans and merchants imported, so that the farmers again are the highest indigenous caste; then come the low castes.

Manu also contrasts the "good people" with the lowest.[3] The division can be traced to the earliest literature

---

[1] There are now claimants to the rank of merchant, co-equal with the farmers, but their claim is suspect. I do not here notice the Vanni caste (found locally on the edge of the jungle, and admitted by the farmers to be slightly higher in rank), because they are known to be later immigrants from India.

[2] For various lists see F. A. Hayley's *Laws and Customs of the Sinhalese* (Colombo, 1922), pp. 89 ff.

[3] X, 38.

where the aristocracy are called *ārya*, that is "worthy," "noble," as opposed to *śūdra*, a term of uncertain origin which may be translated "serf." The aristocracy was distinguished by wearing a sacred thread over the left shoulder, and was subdivided into kings, priests, and farmers. The first two again form an aristocracy within the aristocracy.[1] It has been much debated whether the farmers of Ceylon are the lineal descendants of the original farmer caste, the *vaiśya*, or whether they are a low caste that now finds itself at the head of society owing to the demise of the upper three. Since the Tamil farmers used to admit that they were *śūdra*, and do not wear the sacred thread, the second view seems to be the right one. But this discussion is of no interest for us: this is not a legal argument; we are no more concerned with the question whether the Ceylon farmers are heirs of the body of the ancient farmers or not than the student of the institution of monarchy is concerned with the legitimacy of the House of Hanover; all we need trouble about is whether the Ceylon farmers occupy the place and perform the functions of the old farmer caste or not. This they undoubtedly do, holding such ranks as village headman, and all the offices of state other than the priestly ones, feeding the king and temple, and receiving service from the lower castes. Modern Sinhalese society thus differs from the ancient one only in so far as the aristocracy is single and no longer threefold.

In addition to the four castes Buddhist writings occasionally mention a fifth which is in one place called "low one," as opposed to the exalted one of the kings and priests. This low caste is composed of five divisions: *caṇḍāla*, bamboo-workers, hunters, chariot-makers, scavengers. Manu, on the other hand, declares that there is

[1] For detailed evidence see *Ceylon Journal of Science*, Section G, Vol. I, p. 66. Add *Vinaya*, IV, 6.

no fifth caste, and it is evident that the term "caste" is only applied to this group loosely: they form no part of the four caste system, but lie outside it; and there is no general term for them, so that Buddhist writings have to refer to them by the name of the first division or a compound of the first and last. They are not allowed to dwell in the city or the village, whereas the serfs or artisans have a definite quarter assigned to them. Manu will not allow them a permanent residence at all; and they are called "known by day" because they may not appear in public except in the daytime.[1] In short they lie outside the pale of society with its fourfold division, and they are rightly described by Europeans as outcastes. I am not aware that at the present time any distinction is made in Ceylon between low castes and people outside the caste system, outcastes. Yet, if the term does not exist, the institution does: the Rodiyas are completely outside the pale; they do not, like the barbers, drummers, and the rest, form a necessary part of the social system, fulfilling certain indispensable functions; but they are completely excluded. "They are," says Knox, "to this day so detestable to the People, that they are not permitted to fetch water out of their Wells; but do take their water out of Holes or Rivers. Neither will any touch them lest they should be defiled. . . . They do beg for their living; and that with so much importunity, as if they had a Patent for it from the King, and will not be denied."

We need not insist on the restrictions to which the intercourse between one caste and another is subject, since it is the aspect that has most struck outside observers, and is almost the best known. Thus in the north-central provinces of Ceylon the farmers will not intermarry with the drummers, nor eat with them, not even accept a

[1] *Vinaya*, IV, 6; *Aṅguttara*, I, 162; *Jātaka*, III, 194; *Manu*, IV, 79, XII, 55, X, 51; *Mahāvaṃsa*, X, 92; *Skt. Dict., s.v., divākīrti.*

drink of water from them. They will, on the other hand, eat with the Vanni caste out of the same plate, but the two will not intermarry or attend each other's funerals. There is a case of one-sided intermarriage: the higher will marry women of the lower, but not *vice versa*.[1] These are but commonplace instances. The reader who wishes to follow the fantastic variety of these regulations can do so in the second chapter of the third part of Knox's *Ceylon* and the fourth chapter of M. Senart's book, while we pass on to inquire what it is that the people who actually work the system regard as most fundamental in it.

III

Let us ask them. To the question "What is caste?" a Tamil friend answers: "The castes have a particular work to do for the cultivator. This is how it is generally understood." Another Tamil giving evidence before a commission states that the low castes "were only service classes, such as washermen and barbers. Such low-caste people in olden days were treated by their masters as their own children." A third Tamil gentleman writes: "One thing that ought to be borne in mind is that the Tamil chieftain lived as a feudal lord with all his vassals round about him. He had therefore slaves and vassals to serve him on all occasions, and these slaves and vassals represented different castes who served him in such capacity whenever occasion demanded. The vassals were called *kudimai* and the slaves *adimai*." I will add that *kudimai* is from *kudi*, a house. By vassals therefore my informant means household retainers.

The point of view of rude Sinhalese villagers lost in the jungle of the North Central Province is the same, only they cannot define, they can only illustrate. The farmers

[1] *Halagama* and *Vahunpura*.

of one village make the following statement: "The people of Kadurupiṭiya are drummers. ... They are like servants: when called they must come for dancing, festivals, processions. The farmers give the drummers food on a leaf, also cash for their hard work. When the drummers come for a propitiation ceremony they are given clothes; only then."

Thus, what is uppermost in the minds of all our witnesses is the idea of service: the farmers are feudal lords to whom the others owe certain services, each according to his caste. But what kind of service? To the European the drummers are just men who make a noise on a drum; to a native they are much more than that. This is clearly shown in the polite title by which our farmers referred to the drummers: they did not call them "drummers," as I have rendered it, but "astrologers."[1] For them, clearly, drumming is not the essence of the calling, but only one manifestation of that essence, the other manifestations being dancing and ceremonies known as *bali*. In Sanskrit *bali* means an offering of food to various beings; in Pali an offering to subordinate deities and to demons;[2] but in Ceylon it has connected itself more particularly with planets: if a man is afflicted by a planet, they make a statue of the planet, tie a string to one end and give the other end to the patient; then with appropriate ceremonies the astrologer-drummers rid him of his disease.

Drummers specialize in two directions: there are those who beat the demon drum, and those who beat the temple drum.[3] The demon drummers carry out ceremonies to expel demons; for instance, there is the *tovil* to cure diseases caused by demons,[4] and in the course

---

[1] *Näkaṭi minissu*, from Skt. *nakṣatra*, constellation.

[2] *Yakkha*, e.g. *Mahāvaṃsa*, XXXVI, 88.

[3] *Yakbera* and *singāra gahana minissu*.

[4] *Yaksayo karaṇa leḍa*.

of which the drummers, wearing demon masks, dance and make offerings[1] of the blood of fowls and other animals; the demons are afraid and depart. We now seem to have got at the principle from which the various activities of the drummer are derived: he is primarily a demon-priest, and it is as such that he dances and drums. He identifies himself with his spirits by wearing a mask. This may explain why "the good people" will not beat a drum ceremonially, but have no objection to doing so in play; why it is the work of "the good people" to put on masks and dance at processions, because "they do it in play," but they would not for the world wear masks and dance in a demon ceremony. The drummer is the priest of an inferior cult which the good people use, but do not perform, just as with us respectable people may consult a fortune-teller, but would scorn to be one. To supplicate the demon is one thing, to impersonate him quite another. A respectable person must fear demons because they are connected with death, but for that very reason he must not be identified with them. The connection of demons and planets, and so of drummers, with death is clearly expressed in a Sinhalese poem entitled "Demon-dancing": "The principal thing for this country and for the Sinhalese is the worship of planets. This custom prevails in the world and is appointed to mankind as a painful duty. The representation of the planets *in the burying place* has been made from the beginning."[2]

This view of drummers is confirmed by the distinction the Tamils of Ceylon draw between musicians and drummers. The musicians officiate at temples and on auspicious occasions, such as weddings, ear-borings, house-warmings, and they rank about fifth among castes —that is, fairly high in the scale. The drummers, familiar

[1] *Bili,* the true Sinhalese for Skt. *bali.*
[2] J. Callaway, *Yakkun nattanava,* p. 10.

to us all under the name of Pariahs, officiate at funerals
and sometimes at temples when sacrificial victims are
slaughtered, such a blood-stained worship being considered low. These drummers come last but one.

In conclusion, the drummers are a kind of priests, and
that is why they form a caste, for priesthood is hereditary
in all but a few advanced cults. They are a low caste
because their cult is low, albeit necessary. Let us now see
how far these conclusions explain other castes.

To the European the barber is just a man who shaves
others, the washerman a man who does the laundry. For a
native these two mean much more than that. "Practically
on every occasion," says my first Tamil witness, "the
barber and the washerman will have to be present. They
are called the children of the family."[1] When we analyse
what he means by "occasions" we find that he has in
mind festivals, such as weddings, funerals, etc. Thus at
a Tamil wedding the musicians[2] walk before the bridegroom, the washerman spreads cloths for the bridegroom
(who for the time being is the god Siva) to walk upon.
"In the rear other washermen assisted by barbers sing
or howl (*sic*) blessings and praises of which he [the
bridegroom] is the subject."[3] The barber carries the *tali*
or marriage necklace (the equivalent of our wedding
ring), and the cloth called *kurai* for the bride. What the
bridegroom wears while he is being shaved becomes the
perquisite of the washerman and the barber. At a funeral
the barber, the washerman, and the drummer are sent for,
not the musicians. Men of the domestic servant caste
(*koviyar*) carry the body to the cremation ground. "The
barber prepares the fire for the cremation, and conducts

---

[1] *Kudimakkal.*

[2] *Naduvar*, literally "dancers," as opposed to the drummers.

[3] Arumugam, "Customs and Ceremonies in the Jaffna District," *Ceylon Antiquary*, II (1910), 240.

the person who lights the fire three times round the pyre." "On the completion of each circuit he knocks a hole in the pot" which he holds.[1] In the words of one of my informants "he is like a priest on the cremation ground. The priest who conducts ceremonies in the house does not go to the cremation ground. . . . When the fire is burning the barber takes one or two pieces of bone and keeps them till the thirty-first day ceremony. . . . After pouring water to extinguish the fire, he ploughs the land and sows gingelly and eight kinds of grain." In Travancore the barber has a Sanskrit title which means "one who helps souls, indicating their priestly functions in the ceremonial of various castes."[2] Evidently that is what looms large in the minds of the people, not shaving, which is merely one item in his priestly functions. I shall give another illustration of these from a Bant funeral in Southern India: at the end of it "a washerman touches those who attend with a cloth, and a barber sprinkles water over them. In this manner they are freed from pollution."[3] There are times when a brahman sprinkles water, but not on the cremation ground.

In the words "he is like a priest on the cremation ground" we have the key to the whole problem. The barber and the washerman, like the drummers, are not so much technicians as priests of a low grade, performing rites which the high-caste priest will not touch. The brahman, priest of the immortal gods, can have nothing to do with death. For funeral rites the Tamils of Ceylon have to call in a man of the Śūdra caste who does not eat meat, and who is termed a "Śiva teacher";[4] but even he

[1] Arumugam, "Customs and Ceremonies in the Jaffna District," *Ceylon Antiquary*, II (1910), 244.
[2] The term is *prāṇopakāri* (compare "psychopompos"), E. Thurston, *Tribes and Castes of Southern India*, I, 41.
[3] *Ibid.*, I, 171.
[4] *Saivakkuru*, Skt. *Śaiva* + *guru*.

cannot approach the extreme pollution of the cremation ground, so at this point the barber and the washerman have to take over from him. Because of the pollution involved, the two are low caste.

The barber may be low, but there are lower than he whom he will not shave, and who must therefore have barbers of their own. That is the case of the Chaliyan weavers, and note that their barbers are also their chaplains.[1]

I had for some time been suspecting that the low rank of the washerman had something to do also with the washing away of the menstrual blood, when Mr. M. M. Wedderburn independently put forward the same view, and supported it with the following incident. A Sinhalese police inspector belonging to the washerman caste was sent to investigate a murder. He came to search the suspected house for traces of blood. This annoyed a woman of the house, who was of better caste. She threw at his head a lot of cloth stained with menstrual blood, saying, "There, washerman, are your blood-stained clothes." Indeed, the close association is loudly proclaimed in one of the titles by which the washerman is known. He is addressed as *koṭahaluvā*, "he of the short-cloth"; now, the short-cloth feast is the feast held at the first menses of a girl, when he brings clean clothes and receives as a gift those she wore.[2] He also deals with the pollution of birth, or rather his wife does, for no servant, not even the nurse, will have anything to do with the soiled sheets, but Mrs. Washerman is notified and comes to remove them.

In Ceylon the washerman, like the drummer, appears in demon-worship. According to Parker, the two assistants of the demon priest who dances the dance of the

[1] Thurston, *op. cit.*, II, 11.
[2] See my "Confinement at Puberty," *Man*, 1927, No. 31.

Sinhalese God of the Rock are the washerman who washes his clothes, and the smith who made the god's emblem.[1]

This incidentally brings out the connection of the smiths with the ritual: they make emblems, statues of the gods, temple jewellery. They work also for the family rites by making wedding necklaces, for instance. It is indeed possible that all jewellery began as ritual accessories.

In South India potters sometimes officiate as priests[2] in temples of village goddesses[3] and of the god Aiyanar. They used to make sepulchral urns. Painted hollow clay images are made by special families of potters known as priests, who, for the privilege of making them, have to pay an annual fee to the headman; he spends it on a festival at the caste temple. They make images of the seven virgins for childless couples, ex-votos, horses on which Aiyanar rides down demons. The potters provide the pots which represent the gods at weddings. Even the making of pots for domestic usages has a ritual element, for the potter never begins his day's work at the wheel without forming into a phallus and saluting the revolving lump of clay, which, with the wheel, resembles the symbols of Siva in the temples. In fine, the potter too is a kind of priest, and we need not be surprised when he claims to be of priestly origin, to be descended from Kulālan, the son of Brahmā. He prayed to Brahma to be allowed like him to create and destroy things daily; so Brahmā made him a potter.[4] In Ceylon I was told they wear the sacred thread peculiar to the well born castes "because they claim to be Brahmans: as Brahmā fashioned men, so they fashion pots, images without breath." The potters can quote in their support Buddhist traditions

---

[1] *Ancient Ceylon*, pp. 189, 198.   [2] *Pujari*.
[3] *Pidari*. Thurston, *op. cit.*, III, 189.   [4] Thurston, *s.v. kusavan*.

of a pot-making god Brahmā who was a potter in a former existence, and later became the great priestly god.[1]

If we believe the potters, as everyone seems to do in India, we shall be in a position to understand one of their functions which at first sight seem to have no connection with pot-making: they deal with dislocated bones and all kinds of fractures, leaving boils, wounds, and tumours to the barbers. Now the priests of Vedic times periodically created the world, not indeed its matter, but its essence or force, by fashioning a clay pan which was made equivalent to the world by carefully designed rites and words of power.[2] Things can be renovated, mended, by acting upon a clay images of them, so pot-making and bone-setting go together. Then why should the potter be of inferior status to the brahman? In the words "images without breath" I think we hold the clue. The brahman puts breath, life, into the idol at the ceremony of its consecration, or putting in of the eyes;[3] the potter cannot. He has specialized in the manual side of this operation; he continues to make images and mend men with his hands, while the scholarly brahman continues to mend things by means of the Word. In a country where learning is as arrogant as it is in India, it is not surprising that the potters have sunk while the scholars have soared.

I could go on to show how the carpenters make the temple car in return for grants of land, how Billava toddy-drawers of South Canara officiate as priests at devil shrines, and so go on piling instances on instances;[4] but science does not consist in piling up instances; rather

[1] *Ghaṭīkaramahābrahma* in *Jātaka*, I, 69; *Majjhimanikāya*, II, 45.
[2] *Śat. Brahm.*, VI, 5, 1. Cp. my *Kingship*, 190.
[3] See my article "Idols" in *Encyclopædia of the Social Sciences*.
[4] For more see Thurston, *s.v. ambalavāsi, bhatrāzu*, etc.

it consists in finding the principles underlying a set of
facts; once this has been ascertained beyond doubt there is
no more point in collecting more illustrations of a custom
than there would be in studying the fall of every apple
after the law of gravitation has been established. What we
want is not quantity, but quality: a few decisive facts are
worth tons of indecisive. Can anything be more decisive
than the case of the Sinhalese caste known as "jaggery
men," but more aptly described as cooks?[1] Food in ordinary life is prepared by the housewife or the servants of
whatsoever caste. At the Temple of the Tooth the cook
is a farmer, not a jaggery man. Then where does the
cook caste come in? Ask a Sinhalese: he will tell you they
come to farmers' weddings and other festivals to cook.
The scullion at the Temple of the Tooth is of the cook
caste; but so are the night-watchers, who have nothing to
do with cooking. Evidently cooking is not the essence
of their calling, but menial service in ceremonies and
temples, including kitchen work.[2]

As a last illustration, we may take the *durayā*, or
"servant caste" of Ceylon. They are split up into three
divisions:[3] the first keeps watch, makes triumphal arches,
sweeps, and so forth, at the eight great Buddhist sanc-
tuaries of Anuradhapura; the second performs the same
services at the Temple of the Tooth; the third lives by
doing hired work. Thus the first two are based on temple
service; as for the third, it is not clear, for the occasions
on which such people are called in are not stated in my
information.

We may wind up the argument by pointing out that in

---

[1] Jaggery, *hakuru*, is sugar made from a palm. Mr. S. Paravitana thinks
hakuru, as caste name, is a false etymology from a derivate of Skt. *sūpa-
kāra*, cook.

[2] Hocart, *The Temple of the Tooth in Kandy* (Luzac & Co., 1930),
Chap. III.

[3] *Villi, panna, batgama.*

India every occupation is a priesthood; for the idea that success depends on skill, on the perfection of the mental organization, is comparatively modern; it may not be older than the Greeks. A considerable part of the world still believes that success depends on the help of external powers, gods, demons, or whatever it may be. In order to succeed, therefore, it is most important that the artisan should propitiate those powers. Thus the coolies at a salt factory "never scrape salt from the pans without making a Ganesa [the elephant-headed god, remover of obstacles] of a small heap of salt." The principal object of worship of certain washermen of Mysore is "the pot of boiling water in which dirty clothes are steeped. Animals are sacrificed to the god with a view to preventing the clothes being burnt in the pot." Certain fishermen on a certain day worship the fishing basket and the trident.[1] Business men worship their books once a year, and a friend of mine has seen a dancing girl worship her anklets.

The priestly character of all craftsmen may explain why the Sinhalese smith of the seventeenth century would sit solemnly on a stool, content to hold the iron, and give it now and again a finishing touch, while the customer did the work:[2] he was not so much the man who did the forging as the master of those ceremonies that ensured success in forging. Crafts and rites are not strictly distinguishable, and the Sanskrit word *karma*, "deed," "work," expresses both. The craftsman is, as it were, the man who has the ear of the deity presiding over some particular activity. Heredity is an important, though not the only, qualification for this relation to the deity.

[1] Thurston, IV, 191; I, 17; I, 128.   [2] Knox's *Ceylon*, pp. 67 f.

IV

The conclusion we have arrived at on modern evidence is that the caste system is a sacrificial organization, that the aristocracy are feudal lords constantly involved in rites for which they require vassals or serfs, because some of these services involve pollution from which the lord must remain free.

How far is this conception ancient?

The idea of service is contained in the writings that follow the Vedic period. They are agreed that the royal caste was created for justice, for the protection of the people, and so for war and executive power; the priests for ritual and study; the farmers for cattle-breeding, trade, and cultivation; the serfs for crafts and service.[1]

These texts, like our modern witnesses, do not as a rule give any hint as to the nature of those services, for the excellent reason that they were addressing themselves to an audience to which these services were quite familiar. Books do not set out to tell what everybody knows. Nevertheless the *Visnu Purāna* does definitely state the ritual character of caste. It says that Brahma made this entire fourfold system for the performance of the sacrifice. A practical demonstration of this thesis is given us at the present day by certain castes of South India, the sub-divisions of which are called *bali*, sacrifice; each sub-division is thus a group with common rites, or, as we might put it, a group the members of which are in communion with one another.[2]

The sacrificial basis of caste appears still more clearly when we ascend further back to the old ritual literature.

[1] *Vāyupurāna*, VII, 168 *ff.*; *Bhāgavata Pur.*, III, 6, 29; *Mahābhārata*, Sāntip., 3406; *Visnu Pur.*, I, 36; *Jataka*, III, 208; *Manu*, I, 88.

[2] *Visnu Pur.*, I, 6, 6. Thurston, I, 24.

C

There the worthy or excellent castes are those which alone
are admitted to share in the sacrifice, with whom alone the
gods hold converse.[1] We must not take this to mean that
the craftsmen have no religion, or have a different religion
from the aristocratic castes. Formulæ exist for placing
the sacrificial fire of the chariot-maker.[2] But the ritual
books are not concerned with religion in general and the
rites of all classes, but mainly with the state sacrifices,
such as the king's consecration, the priest's installation,
and so forth. The main object of these sacrifices was the
pursuit of immortality, not immortality as we understand
it, but freedom from premature death and the diseases
that cause it and the renewal of this vigorous life hereafter.
"This is the immortality of man," says one authority,
"that he reaches a complete life." And again, "Immortality endless, unbounded, is as much as a hundred
years."[3] It is a very concrete and immediate immortality.
It is to be secured by becoming a god and ascending to
the world of the gods. In the words of the teacher, "The
sacrificer passes from men to the gods." The way in
which this is effected is explained thus: "The sacrifice is
the other self of the gods; ... therefore the sacrificer having
made the sacrifice his other self takes his place in this sky,
this heavenly world."[4] In other words the process is:

$$sacrifice = gods;$$
$$sacrificer\ becomes = sacrifice;$$
$$\therefore\ sacrificer\ becomes = gods.$$

As vehicles of the immortal gods (immortal in the sense
of possessing the full life) the members of the three

[1] *Śat. Brāhm.*, III, 1, 1, 9 *f.*

[2] Macdonell and Keith, *Vedic Index*, II, 253, referring to *Taitt., Brāh.*,
I, 1, 4, 8.

[3] *Śat Brāhm.*, IX, 5, 1, 10; X, 2, 1, 4; cp. X, 2, 6, 7. Hence the greeting,
"Live a hundred years," *Jāt.*, I, 35. *Śat. Brāhm.*, II, 5, 1, 7; X, 2, 6, 4.

[4] *Śat. Brāhm.*, VIII, 6, 1, 10.

excellent castes may not come into contact with death and that which leads to death—namely, decay and disease. Such a contact would impair their full life on which the life of the community depends.

If one section may not concern itself with the in-auspicious ritual of death for fear of contaminating the auspicious ritual of life, then some other section must handle death and decay, for these are inexorable facts which must be dealt with. A hereditary group is therefore necessary to deal with them. These men are the serfs, the *śūdras* of later writings, the *dasyu* or *dāsa* of the Rig-veda. They are not in communion with the gods; they were not created simultaneously with the gods like the higher castes;[1] on the contrary, they are demons, *asura*, the powers of darkness.[2]

It seems monstrous to the modern mind that a whole section of the community should be identified with the powers of evil; therefore the modern mind refuses to take such statements seriously. "Merely priestly arrogance," it is said. But we have seen at the present day Sinhalese drummers, serfs of the "good people," impersonating demons, and on that account taking no part in the Buddhist ritual which is the heir of the old brahmanic state ritual. It is only natural that those who "are priests on the cremation ground" should be representatives of the powers of darkness and death.

It will be easier for us to admit the literal truth of the statements of early writers if we remember that our word "demon" is not a satisfactory translation of the words *asura* and *yaksha*: there is too much of wickedness in it. The *asura* are not evil incarnate, like our devils: they are merely the powers of darkness which are evil only in so far as they encroach too much on light. We should

[1] *Taitt. Saṃh.*, VII, 1, 1, 4 *ff.*
[2] *Pañcaviṃśa*, V, 5, 17. *Taitt. Brāhm.*, I, 2, 6, 7.

perhaps come nearer the truth if we described *deva*
and *asura* as light god and dark god. There is not even a
strict line of demarcation, for the sun is called an *asura*,
just as Apollo is called a Titan.[1] Perhaps we might speak
of "gods" and "titans": it would be historically correct,
for the Titans of the Greeks and the *asura* of the Indians
are certainly derived from a common stem. A god may be
partly a titan, Soma, for instance who is also Vṛtra.[2]
In the same way the human representatives of titans can
also represent gods: thus the serfs are identified with
titans, but also with the god Pūṣan "the kinsman of
heaven and earth."[3] They represent gods in certain
episodes of the ritual. In the king's consecration certain
court officials belonging to the fourth caste (for serfdom
is not inconsistent with important office near the king)
take a walking on part, as it were; they do so as gods, even
such great gods as Rudra. And yet, even though they
stand for gods, their presence causes the king "to enter
darkness," as the sun "stricken with darkness" by the
demon "does not shine." The king therefore has to
offer a pap to the gods Soma and Rudra that they may
"repel that darkness of his."[4]

V

In conclusion, castes are merely families to whom
various offices in the ritual are assigned by heredity.

That is merely the theory which the ancient texts have
dinned into the deaf ears of nineteenth-century scholars.
Bred with a rationalistic, anti-priestly bias, these scholars
have consistently rejected this theory as nothing but an

---

[1] *Ṛgv.*, I, 35, 10. *C.*, I, 2,342.
[2] *Śat. Brāhm.*, III, 4, 3, 13 *ff.*
[3] *Ibid.*, XIV, 4, 2, 23. *Ṛgv.*, VI, 58, 4.
[4] *Śat. Brāhm.*, V, 3, 2, 2. *Kingship*, 113 *ff.*

invention of the priests in order to spread their tentacles through the social fabric. We have seen the theory, however, held quite as strongly by peasants and others quite free from all priestly taint. It is a popular view of caste.

We can now take up our ancient texts with greater confidence in their veracity.

Rigveda, X, 90, expresses this theory by making caste proceed from the sacrifice. It is curious that this formulation should have been treated as fantastic theology, when *Manu* has told us very clearly in what sense the castes are born of the ritual. He has shown us every youth of good family going through the ritual of initiation, as the result of which he is reborn as a member of his father's caste. This is not fantastic theology, but a common process not confined to India, but found all over the world. Every son of a brahman is born of his father, but he is also born of the sacrifice, and so is every *kṣatriya* and every farmer. Hence such expressions as "the first-born of prayer" (*Rgv.*, III, 29, 15), "twice-born, first-born of the ritual" (*Rgv.*, X, 61, 19. Cp. II, 144, 17; I, 164, 37).

This type of myth is not confined to the priests. Telugu bangle-makers believe that their caste is born of the sacrifice, and therefore they call themselves *Balija*, "Born of the Offering." They describe this birth in the following manner: "Pārvatī was not satisfied with her appearance when she saw herself in the looking-glass, and asked her father to tell her how she was to make herself more attractive. He accordingly prayed to Brahma, who ordered him to perform a severe penance. From the sacrificial fire kindled in connection therewith, arose a being leading a donkey laden with heaps of bangles, turmeric, palm-leaf rolls for ears, black beads, sandal powder, a comb, perfumes, etc. To this Great

Man [*mahāpuruṣa*] in token of respect were given flags, torches, and certain musical instruments."[1]

Such a myth is invariably rejected as historically worthless, because it is physically impossible. It is not so. Causing men to pass through fire, scorching them on a heap of brushwood, and other forms of fictitious cremation are an essential episode of many initiation ceremonies which cause a man to be reborn.[2] It is perfectly possible then for a man to be reborn as bangle-maker, as the result of passing through fire. If it appears impossible to us, that is due to our ignorance: we may know physics, but we do not know the customs of the world.

The evidence of *Rigveda*, X, 90, is often brushed aside on the ground that it is a late hymn; but the *argumentum a silentio* is a dangerous one: the first appearance of a custom in the texts is seldom, if ever, its first appearance in the world. It often is not recorded until it begins to decay. In this case there is not even silence: we have quoted from earlier books to show that the idea of rebirth from the sacrifice existed before book X.

How much older? India alone can never answer that question: it will take us back as far as the Rigveda and leave us there. If we wish to get beyond, we must resort to comparative evidence, as did the philologists when they wanted to get back beyond the dialects of the Vedas and of Homer to the parent tongue.[3]

The comparative evidence lies outside the scope of this paper: I hope to deal with it exhaustively in some other papers. In the meantime, I can only anticipate it by warning the reader that myths of the type of *Rigveda*,

---

[1] Thurston, *s.v. Balija. Mahāpuruṣa* is the sacrificial victim in *Rgv.*, X, 90.

[2] See my *Kingship*, XII, and my *Progress of Man*, 151, 158 f. Quaritch Wales, "Theory and Ritual connected with Pregnancy, etc.," *Journ. Roy. Anthr. Inst.*, 1933, 441.

[3] See my *Kings and Councillors*, I.

X, 90, are not confined to India. They are world-wide. They mostly describe the creation of the world and man in general, but sometimes they account for the divisions of the people, somewhat on the lines of the *Viṣṇu Purāṇa*, I, 6, 6, and of *Manu*, I, 87*ff.*,[1] only in a more matter of fact way, since they are popular, not learned versions. The gist of them is that the ancestor, the god, at his installation assigns to each branch of his family in the order of seniority the duties it will have to perform in the state ceremonial.[2]

We are faced with two alternatives: either all these myths were derived from India after the composition of the Purusa hymn, or else that hymn is merely the Indian version of a much older myth, older than the Aryan culture of India. The first alternative does not appear to fit the facts, so we are left with the second.

To return to India, our next task is to show that the details of its caste system fit in perfectly well with the theory which makes it an organization for ritual, that the alleged inconsistencies are misunderstandings on our part, misunderstandings which spring, like our disbelief in the legend of the *Balija*, from our ignorance of living institutions; for when we examine these we shall find that they fully corroborate the ancient texts, and that India has not changed as much as is often supposed.

VI

Let us begin with the skeleton of the system, the four-fold grouping of the population in *kshatriya*, *brahman*, *vaiśya*, *śudra*. This, we are constantly told, bears no

---

[1] Or *Śat. Brāhm.*, II, i, 4, 11: "The creator created the earth and the corresponding brahman caste by saying '*bhūḥ*,' the air and the nobility by saying '*bhuvah*,' the heavens and the farmers by saying 'sky.' "

[2] Cp. *Kingship*, Chap. XVI.

resemblance to reality. The reality is to be found in Indian censuses, in the dictionaries of castes and tribes, and in the daily experience of Indian civil servants. What do we find there? Not four castes, but an infinitude, with an endless variety of customs, of mutual relations, and even of racial types. Therefore the four-caste system is a pure figment, the invention of priests for their own glorification.

Before we apply an argument to a people whose ways are remote and little known (for, in spite of all the books about it, India remains an unknown country), before we take such risks it is well to test the argument on our own society which we do know. Our constitution divides the people into lords and commons. When, however, we examine the reality we find that the lords are a collection of families of different ranks—dukes, marquesses, and so on. We can also distinguish among them different sets which have little to do with one another. We can even distinguish different racial types, notably the Jewish. Among the commons the variety is even greater: it ranges from baronets, who come near to being peers, down to horny-handed navvies. Do we on that account reject the classification into lords and commons as a figment of our constitutional theorists? Why, we can see them any day sitting in separate houses with different procedures and privileges. It is a theory, but it is a theory translated into practice. Such is any social organization.

Why then should an Indian classification of the people into four be unreal because it gathers together into one group such heterogeneous elements as barbers, mat-makers, and sometimes even aborigines? Why should not such a classification be just as important in the state as ours? As a matter of fact, it is much more important since it runs through the daily life of the masses.

We saw that in Ceylon the leading caste is now the

farmer caste. All the members of that caste are not equal; there are within it mutually exclusive groups, there are aristocratic ones that will not intermarry with the less aristocratic; but however much their status may vary, it is constant in one particular—that they are the feudal lords as contrasted with the retainers who owe them service. Certain offices and titles too are reserved to them. Thus a title ending in *rāḷa* (which formerly meant "king") indicates an office reserved for farmers.[1] Not every such office is open to any farmer. It may be confined to a particular house. Thus the office of steward, *vaṭṭerurāḷa*, at the Temple of the Tooth is of farmer rank as indicated by the termination, but it is specially reserved for two families of farmer rank, Aladeniya and Aludeniya. Even so *we* have court functions which can only be carried out by a peer, but within the peerage they are claimed by certain families.

In the same way, there are offices which are low caste, but they are not open to any man of low birth. A barber or a washerman could not come and drum at the temple; only a drummer can do so, and not every drummer, but only the descendants of those to whom the king assigned lands on a service tenure.

If we examine the various offices at the Temple of the Tooth and try and discover some line that divides high from low, we shall find that:

1. All those that officiate inside the sanctuary are farmers. It is significant that the drummers who play in the courtyard are low, but the singers who come and sing on the balcony of the sanctuary are farmers. These singers accompany themselves with drum, tambourines and cymbals. Evidently it is not the drum that is the cause of lowness.[2]

2. Authority lies with the farmers, menial duties with

[1] *Temple of the Tooth*, 11.   [2] *Ibid.*, 13; 17.

the low castes. Thus the cook is a farmer, his scullion a member of the so-called cook caste. The watchers are cooks, but the sergeant of the watch is a farmer.[1]

The priests do not form a caste. Being celibates they cannot found families. They must, however, be drawn from the farmer caste, and at the Temple of the Tooth from aristocratic families within that caste.[2] They have usurped in the ritual the place held by the brahmans when priesthood was hereditary.

The worship is addressed to the Buddha, son of a king, born to be king. The scriptures never weary of his royal birth; he is known as "The *Kshatriya*." The priests in Kandy tell us that the ritual is modelled on the ritual which centres in a king.[3] This is confirmed by what fragments we possess of the court ritual.[4] We thus work back to the following scheme:

Caste		*Office*	
Good People	⎧ Royal ⎨ Priestly ⎩ Farming	Inside	⎧ Receiver of cult ⎨ Celebrant ⎩ Officials
Low:	Various		Outside and menial duties

This scheme comes remarkably near to that which is laid down in the old texts:

Caste		*Office*	
Worthy, Sacrificial[5]	⎧ Royal ⎨ Priestly ⎩ Farming	Admitted	⎧ Representative of ⎨ Indra ⎨ Celebrants ⎩ Purveyors of food
Serfs			Excluded except for certain rites.

---

[1] *Temple of the Tooth*, 12.   [2] *Ibid.*, 14.   [3] *Ibid.*, 3, 18, 21.
[4] Sir John D'Oyly, *A Sketch of the Constitution of the Kandyan Kingdom* (Colombo, 1929), pp. 132 *f.*
[5] *Ārya, yajñiya.*

Thus a study of the reality which we can observe with our eyes and ears leads us to a social arrangement which tallies with the supposed unrealities of the texts.

We can therefore confidently accept the ancient classification of castes as based on actual practice. We see it not only in the ritual, but in the planning of the city. The four groups are placed at different points of the compass within the square or circular city: royal to the east, mercantile to the south, servile to the west, priestly to the north. Heretics and outcastes live outside the city near the cremation ground, the place of corruption.[1] That castes were segregated into quarters is proved by the names of streets such as "brahman street," "merchant street."[2]

VII

If the ancient texts describe actuality, why have we been led to call them in question? The answer is in the first place that the nineteenth century and early twentieth became so intoxicated with their critical sense that they came to believe they knew more about the ancients than the ancients themselves. Secondly, they were so obsessed by certain theories about class distinctions that, if the facts did not agree, it was the facts that had to yield.

It was a settled conviction that all aristocracies were due to conquest. Therefore the Indian aristocracy was due to conquest. The aristocracy were the invaders from the North; the serfs were the aboriginal population. They saw in the technical term for the four classes a complete vindication of their theory. That term is *varṇa*, colour.

[1] Kautilya, *Arthaṣastra*, II, 3 *f.*

[2] The meagre archæological evidence has been summed up in *C.J.Sc.*, G, II, 86 *f.*

That, they argued triumphantly, shows that there was a difference of colour between the aristocracy and the serfs. Further, the colour of the serfs is black; the colour of the aboriginal races of India is black. Q.E.D. It was in vain that the ancient authorities told us that the colours were symbolic and connected with the four cardinal points; their statements were brushed aside as mere phantasy. Yet their interpretation was quite simple and straightforward: we know that the four groups were connected with the four quarters, and we know that each quarter has its colour. Why should not each group have a standard, or turban, or robe of its own colour? Where is the difficulty?

On the other hand, the modern theory slurs over serious difficulties. It harps on the black colour of the serfs, and ignores the fact that there is not one aristocratic colour, but three—to wit, red, white, yellow. To be consistent, we should have to suppose that Indian society was a compound of four races, that some unknown red race had established itself on the throne, that white invaders assumed priestly functions, and that the Mongolians took to farming and trade! You cannot pick out one fact that agrees with your theory and leave out the rest: that is not science.

The controversy between the ancients and the moderns might go on indefinitely so long as it is fought on Indian soil alone, for the institutions described in the texts have altered and many features have faded out, so that the statements of the ancients are often unintelligible: we may be able to translate every word, but the subject of the conversation is not understood. It is outside India that we may find the key.

Comparative evidence at once decides in favour of the ancients, for it can produce examples, from Palestine to America, of camps or cities divided into four quarters according to the points of the compass.[1] But it is the Poncas that specially interest us, because they connect each quarter of the camp with one of the four elements.[2] Further south and in China we find each of these four elements linked up with a point of the compass, a season, and a colour. The connection of quarter, colour, social division, season and element is therefore not peculiarly brahmanic, or even Indian, nor is it purely academical, unless our peerage and commons are. Even Europe has its contribution to make: medieval Ferrara was divided into four wards and four suburbs, each with its colours and banners. Medievalists would no doubt have a great deal more to say about it since the doctrine of the four quarters was highly developed at one time in Europe.[3]

Finally, red and yellow are royal colours over a considerable part of the world—for instance, in Cambodia.[4]

VIII

"But," says the critic, "what about those passages of the *Rigveda* which speak of a black skin?" There is I, 130, 8: "Indra, hundred times protecting, favours in the encounters the sacrificing noble in all fights, in heaven-winning fights. Punishing the impious, he subjects the black skin to man." That seems decisive enough. As usual, it only seems decisive as long as we lift this sentence out of the whole system of thought, and consider it in itself. It is as if we tried to interpret Iago's "green-eyed monster" without any reference to the theory of colours, passions and temperaments of Shakespeare's day. Let us

[1] *Kings and Councillors*, XIX. Compare the Hebrew camp, Num. ii, iii, vii, x. Also Baghdad.
[2] J. O. Dorsey, "Siouan Sociology," *Ann. Ry. Bureau of American Ethnology*, 1893-4, 230 *f*.
[3] *Kings and Councillors*, 253.
[4] A. Leclère, *Cambodge*.

put back the term "black skin" into the context to which it belongs.

The three aristocratic castes are regarded as representatives of the gods, who are heavenly, creatures of light, and therefore "ruddy in hue." The very next stanza shows us clearly the meaning of these colours. "When born he set in motion the wheel of the sun with might. At break of day he, ruddy in hue, appropriates the word . . . conquering as by man all glories." In the same way, the Gandharvas, creatures of light, are "sun-skinned."[1] Naturally the giants are "black things."[2] To this day the Sinhalese paint the eastern god yellow, in the north the god is red, in the south green, while Vishnu, who guards the west, is blue, a colour interchangeable with black. No one has ever discovered a blue or a green race. These are the colours, not of races, but of gods, and the context makes it quite plain that it is a battle of gods and giants that is described in the *Rigveda*. The epithet "heaven-winning" alone should make that clear; failing that, the next stanza, which describes the god who sets in motion the sun as victorious over darkness. In the seventh stanza we learn that one of Indra's foes is Śambara, a demon, and that the weapon of victory is the thunderbolt.

As usual, comparative evidence has to be called in to strike the decisive blow in a contest which might go on indefinitely, if confined to Indian soil.

The tribe of Seaṅgāṅgā in Fiji is divided into Red Bodies and Black Bodies. There can be no question of two different races, black and brown, since Black Body always marries Red, and *vice versa*. A Black Body has as much red in him as black, and is only called black on account of his mother. The terms have nothing to do with the skin. Perhaps a clue may be found in the universal practice in Fiji of blackening the face with soot for war, of daubing it

---

[1] *Sūryatvac, Atharvaveda*, II, 2, 2.   [2] *Rgv.*, IV, 16, 13.

with red turmeric for dances unconnected with war. The colours are pigments of life and death. It is significant that they are derived from the ancestral goddesses.

The racial theory has simply picked and chosen what fitted in with the theory of conquest and omitted the rest. That is not science. Social systems must be taken as a whole and explained as a whole. The texts give us a consistent system which was once rejected because it seemed contrary to the facts of Nature. Now that we know more about the social systems and theories of the world, we can see that everything the texts tell us is realized somewhere.

In the Indian variety of this social scheme society is divided into two: one associated with the upper regions over which the gods preside; and so their colours are bright—red for the rising sun, yellow for the sun in the south, and white for the diffused light of the north. The other side is associated with the giants, powers of darkness, and so they dwell in the west, the region of death, and their colour is the colour of death, black or blue.[1]

The bright half is subdivided into three according to the part assigned to them in the ritual of life, which is also light.

The gods and the giants are in perpetual strife, and so therefore are their followers. This may seem incredible until we find over a considerable part of the world—nowhere more clearly than in America—standing contests between the sky people and the earth people, members of the same tribe.

Undoubtedly there was an invasion of India from the north-west which brought in an Aryan dialect. We should expect from the analogy of other conquests that the invaders enrolled the original inhabitants *mainly*

[1] The funeral bridge is on the west side of a Burmese city: *Ref. A.S.I.*, 1902-3, 95.

among the serfs. It so happens that a large proportion of the population they found there, especially in the region south of the country where the *Rigveda* was composed, was dark in colour. That fitted in well with the theology, but did not prompt it. We do not paint the devil black in imitation of Negroes, but we imagine that the Negroes are black because they are the creation of the devil. We did not institute slavery when we came into contact with Negroes, but we fitted the Negroes into a pre-existing system of slavery because they were black and heathens, and so were not entitled to the status of free Christian men.

Each of the four divisions of Indian society is placed within the city at the point of the compass which, for some reason or other, is appropriate: the powers of darkness in the quarter of death, the king towards the rising sun which prevails over darkness. Why the priests should be in the north and the farmers in the south is not clear, but it is a fact to this day that the Sinhalese priests dwell on the right of the temple as you go in. As the temple normally faces east, they normally dwell to the north.[1]

Each social division also corresponds to one of four æons that recur in cycles, and of which each has its colour and its point of the compass. The question of æons is, however, an obscure one, though not insoluble by comparative evidence.[2]

Since each division is known by its colour, it is called a colour. The modern literature on the subject gives the impression that this is the usual and fundamental word for caste. That is the fault of the racial theory. The usual word is *jāti*. *Jāti* means birth, and so lineage. The question

---

[1] *Temple of the Tooth*, 39, and plans in Vol. I of the *Mem. A.S.C.*

[2] A clue is given us by the North American division into summer and winter folk, each side being in charge of the rites of its season. The æons are undoubtedly based on the seasons.

which we (unfortunately) translate "What is his caste?" means simply: "What is his birth, lineage?" We should come nearer to the meaning if we translated the answer, "He is of good birth," instead of "He is of good caste." The term *jāti* has much wider and looser a meaning than we have put upon the Portuguese creation "caste." It does not refer to any particular kind of division or grouping, but simply to hereditary status. In England a man may be of gentle birth, or may describe his status more narrowly by saying he is a peer by birth, or narrow it still further to baron or earl. In the same way you can assign a Sinhalese in a wide way to the people of good birth, or more precisely to those of farmer birth, or particularize whether among farmers he is of higher or lower birth. If he is not a Sinhalese, he may be of Tamil or of Telugu birth.

Different births or lineages may be grouped together according to function. Thus lineages which officiate in the brahmanic ritual are all labelled "brahman"—that is, priestly. The different lineages may possibly not intermarry or have anything to do with one another, but their status is priestly. Even so the aristocracies of England and Japan do not intermarry, or even know one another, but they recognize each other as occupying corresponding places each in its own society, as "homologues," if we can use a biological term.

The ancients collected all the lineages together into four main groups each with its colour and its station. This grouping is naturally no longer as clear cut as it once was, because it is an organization proper to small agricultural states, and its nearest relations are still to be looked for among agricultural or hunting tribes. Since the ancient texts were written empires and big cities have broken up the feudal system, and wiped out many features, such as the colours, the orientation, the seasonal rotation, and so

D

on. To doubt that these features existed once, because they do not exist now, is like denying that snakes ever had legs because they have not got them now.

We can now proceed to study each of these four "colours" in detail and discover the functions on which they are based.

IX

It has become a tradition to describe the *kshatriya* caste as a warrior caste. Later writings lay great stress on this side of its activities, and it fitted in very well with the theory of race and conquest; the other side did not, and so it was ignored. Yet it is the one that appears almost exclusively in the earliest prose writings. Thus we arrive at the strange result that a selection from late statements is preferred as evidence to the entirety of the earliest statements. Surely we want very strong reasons to set aside the earlier in favour of the later. Until such strong reasons have been given we must presume that the earlier writings depict an earlier social organization.

We can perhaps best sum up the first caste as the one that provides the king. It is equally so in the earliest texts and in late inscriptions.[1] Forgeries are the best evidence: kings not of *kshatriya* descent sooner or later forge themselves a *kshatriya* pedigree.[2] Kings should properly come from that caste. We can therefore speak of this caste as the royal one or as the nobility. As such, it is entitled to the royal colour.

In the earliest texts the king appears as "the sacrificer"[3] in the state sacrifice.[4] That does not mean that he controls

[1] *Sat. Br.*, V, 4, 3, 14 and 7 *et passim. Ep. Z.*, II, 64; IV, 65.

[2] E.g. S. Paranavitana, "Two Royal Titles," *J.R.A.S.*, 1936, 443.

[3] *Yajamāna. Yajaman* is still the title of weaver headmen in Mysore. Thurston, III, 129.

[4] *Mhbh., Santi*, 2,280 *f.* Muir, 370.

the ritual, but that he is the chief actor, supplies the offerings, and bears the expense. The difference between him and the priest is summed up thus: "A nobleman gives but does not solicit; offers sacrifice, but does not perform it; studies, but does not teach." Sacrifice is, however, the king's chief duty. Even in the later literature his chief task is to perform, among other things, "the rites of the royal consecration and the horse-sacrifice."[1]

The sacrificer is much more than a worshipper, as we understand the term. He represents a god or gods, more particularly Indra: we are told so not once, but again and again. The king is Indra in a double capacity: firstly, because the sacrificer is always Indra and the king is a sacrificer; secondly, because Indra is the god of his caste. Everything he does in the ritual is as representative of Indra, and all that is done to him is done to Indra. He is, as it were, a living idol, and his place may be taken by an idol of wood or stone, as in the Buddhist ritual.

Indra is primarily a fighting god. The success of the sacrifice is continually threatened by the wiles of the giants. Indra and the other gods have to defeat them so that prosperity may be won. The king as Indra renews in every sacrifice the contest between the light-bringing gods and the powers of darkness, and drives away the giants by the same spells and rites as once stood Indra in good stead.[2]

Just as the gods are impersonated, so are the giants. The king and the other worthy people stand for the gods; the serfs, who do not belong to the communion, represent the powers of darkness. By the correct performance of the rites the sacrificer "slays his evil, hostile adversary."[3]

[1] *Nala*, I, 4.

[2] *Sat. Br.*, IX, 2, 3, 2 *f. et passim*. "Two Vedic Hymns," *C.J.Sc.*, I, 133. *Kingship*, III. *Kings and Councillors*, XI.

[3] *Sat. Br.*, XII, 7, 3, 4 *et passim*.

If the giants have representatives in the flesh there is a very simple and direct way of defeating them and that is by smiting them in the flesh with material weapons. Thus the king fights evil with both carnal and spiritual weapons, as we should express it, and the serf, as the enemy, "can be slain at will."[1]

Not only the serfs, but all those who stand outside the communion, members of nations that worship other gods, represent the demons. The king wages war on "the assembly that does not hold *soma* sacrifices,"[2] the many who commit great sin."[3] The Rigveda is full of the triumph of Indra over "the slave race."[4] It is quite impossible to say how far these battles are waged in the field or on the sacrificial ground. That is equally characteristic of the prayers of medieval Europe.[5] Neither the Vedic nor the medieval mind made a distinction, because there was none. The essential was the fight against the powers of evil, whether these powers were represented by a piece of lead or human beings.[6]

One consequence of the Indian doctrine is that war has became the sport of kings, and that is how the royal caste has come to be a military one. Fighting is not a primary attribute, but only a derivative.

The king has other duties besides fighting. He is other gods besides Indra. He is also Varuna, the god who regulates the world both physical and moral, the lord of law, the guardian of order, whose ordinances all the

---

[1] *Ait. Br.*, VII, 29.

[2] *Rgv.*, VIII, 14, 15.

[3] *Ibid.*, II, 12, 10.

[4] *Ibid.*, I, 12, 4.

[5] *Coronation Book of Charles V*. Cp. *Kingship*, 97.

[6] Have we really changed much? We speak of fighting communism or fascism. Only the context can make it clear whether we mean banning books, preaching the right doctrine, or shooting down the other side. The essential is that the doctrines should be smothered.

gods follow.[1] He is consequently a judge as well as a warrior, and remains so throughout Indian history. The whole prosperity of his people depends upon his *dharma* —that is, his observance of the established order of things. For here again the physical and the spiritual are not yet separated. The laws of Nature and the laws of the State are of the same kind. Varuna is in charge of both, and so perforce is the king, making rain in due season and keeping the peace among his subjects.

There are other *kshatriya* gods: Soma, Rudra, Parjanya, Yama. The king is identified with them also, and even with priestly gods, such as Brahma.[2]

The king does not rear cattle like the farmers.[3] His attribute is the *kshatra* which we can render approximately by the Roman *imperium*.

X

The second caste supplies the priests, brahmans, who perform the ritual for the king or for whatever great man is offering the sacrifice. Just as the king is identified with the royal gods, so is the priest with the priestly gods, Brahma, Brihaspati, Agni, Speech. Agni is the sacrificial fire. Speech is so important in ritual that they say "the sacrifice is speech."[4] Sometimes a priest may be the sacrificer, notably when he is installed in a priestly office;[5] but he is first and foremost the man who officiates for the sacrificer. As such he is more closely related to the royal caste than to the farmers, since the king is the chief

[1] *Rgv.*, I, 23, 5; VIII, 41, 7.
[2] *Manu*, V, 96. *Sat. Br.*, V, 4, 4, 9; II, 3, 2, 6: VII, 1, 1, 4; V, 2, 2, 13 *ff*.
[3] *Sat. Br.*, XIII, 2, 9, 8.
[4] *Ibid.*, II, 4, 1, 10. Cp. *Rgv.*, I, 164, 35. Below Page.
[5] At the *vājapeya* for priests.

sacrificer. Royalty and priesthood form a pair.[1] As usual, the world of gods reflects the world of men, and *vice versa*. Priestly gods unite with royal gods to form compounds such as Indragni, Indrabrihaspati, Agnisoma.[2] This pairing is conceived as that of man and wife: "Then Indragni were created, the priesthood and the sovereignty, for the priesthood is Agni, the sovereignty is Indra. These two, when created, were separate. They said, 'As we cannot procreate offspring let the two of us be one form.' The two became one form."[3] Of Mitravaruna it is said, "Mitra spills semen into Varuna."[4] Like the queen, the chaplain is part of the king's self.[5]

Man and wife are heaven and earth, so are king and priest. The royal gods are celestial, more especially solar. The priestly gods are their counterparts. Thus in the couple Mitravaruna "Mitra is this earthly world, Varuna yon heavenly world."[6] Agni is the earthly representative of the sun: "he is to men what the sun is to the gods."[7] As impersonators of these gods, the brahmans are entitled "earth-gods."[8]

The identity of priest and priestly god is carried out in detail. The fire is the intermediary between sky and men, the priest between king and men. The fire is the messenger of the gods and also leads the gods

---

[1] *Sankh.*, I, 1, 1, 3, quoted by A. Weber, *Indische Studien*, X, 11.

[2] *Sat. Br.*, I, 6, 3, 14 *ff.*; II 4, 4, 10. *Maitr. Samh.*, II, 1, 12. *Rgv.*, VII, 61.

[3] *Sat. Br.*, X, 4, 1, 5 *f.*

[4] *Ibid.*, II, 4, 4, 19.

[5] *Ait. Br.*, VII, 25. Cp. *Sat. Br.*, V, 3, 1, 10. In *Man*, 1927, 92, Professor J. H. Hutton tells us that the founder of a Naga village in Assam must have a companion, "as it were man and wife."

[6] *Sat. Br.*, XII, 9, 2, 12.

[7] *Ibid.*, II, 4, 2, 1 *ff.*; cp. XIII, 6, 1, 9.

[8] E. W. Hopkins, *Epic Mythology*, 64 (In *Grundriss der Indo-Arischen Philologie*, III).

to the sacrifice; therefore he always goes in front; he is the face of the deities.[1] Even so, the king's chaplain is called *purohita,* placed in front, and he "goes before the king."[2]

The insignia of the priest is the staff, as the sword is of the king.[3]

XI

About the third caste, the *viś,*[4] whom I have called farmers, we hear but little, because they are neither chiefs nor scholars. They *presumably* function as sacrificers in the ceremonies by which they are consecrated to the offices that belong to them; but these are minor events of which we hear little or nothing. We should hardly look to the works of bishops and canons for information about the social position and religious activities of our farmers.

The farmer caste follows the general rule that all those who take any part in the ritual must represent gods; but they have this peculiarity: that they do not represent single gods, as do the king and the priest, but whole groups, "those kinds of gods that are referred to in bands, such as the Vasus, Adityas, All-gods, Maruts."[5] Thus *Rudra* is the sovereignty; he is a royal god, but the minor *rudras* sprung from Prajapati's tears are the farmers.[6] The reason has, as usual, to be sought for in the social realities: there is one king, one chaplain, but there

---

[1] *Rgv.,* V, 11, 4; I, 1, 2; I, 188, 11. *Sat. Br.,* V, 3, 1, 1.

[2] *Ibid.,* IV, 50, 8.

[3] *Ramayana, Balakanda,* 56, 4 (Muir, I, 399). Cp. *Kingship,* 24, 138.

[4] An earlier name seems to be *krishthi. Rgv.,* I, 4, 6.

[5] *Sat. Br.,* XIV, 4, 2, 24.

[6] *Ibid.,* XI, 5, 1, 12; X, 4, 1, 9; II, 4, 3, 6; IX, 1, 1, 15; X, 4, 1, 9; XIV, 4, 2, 23 *f.*

are many chieftains.[1] We have already observed this fact at the Temple of the Tooth: one king, one priest, and several lay officers of farmer status.[2] These lay officers are mainly concerned with preparing and bringing the food. It is also from lands of farmers that the temple is provided with food for presentation to the spiritual king.[3] Thus present custom gives us a clue to the obscure old texts which say that "the king is an eater, the yeomanry food"; "the yeomanry is another's tributary, another's food"; "whatever belongs to the yeomanry, the nobleman has a share in it."[1] Our word tributary renders but ill the original *balikrit*, which means literally "maker of offerings."[4]

The farmers then are the support on which the monarch and the priesthood rest, and their duty is to feed the sacrifice from their lands and cattle.

The gods of the farmers, the Maruts, act as Indra's bodyguard. Since divine society is a replica of human society, we must conclude that the farmers are the king's mainstay in battle. They are just as military then as the nobles.

[1] *Sat. Br.*, IX, 3, 1, 14.

[2] In the main shrine there is a second priest, but he is not necessary and comes out for part of the service. His presence is probably due to that duplication of office which is so common in the Sinhalese state. Hocart, "Duplication of Office in the Indian State," *C.J.Sc.*, G, I, 205.

[3] D'Oyly, 20, 44.

[4] *Sat. Br.*, VI, 1, 2, 25; XI, 2, 7, 16; IX, 1, 1, 18; VIII, 7, 1, 2. *Ait Br.*, VII, 9. *Kings and Councillors*, 206.

XII

We thus arrive at the following social scheme:

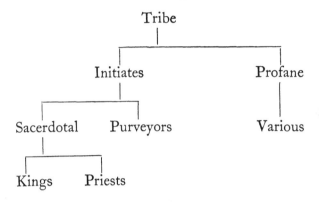

Since the serfs are excluded from the sacrifice, we do not expect to hear much of them in books devoted to the sacrifice. Yet they do play an occasional, though necessary, part. Nor must it be imagined that they are destitute of ritual. We know that formulæ existed for placing the sacrificial fire of the chariot-maker who is not included among the "worthy" people.[1] In ancient Ceylon the artificer god might enter a builder and inspire him.[2] We must conclude that, like the present-day low castes, they had their own cult and were "impious" only in the sense that they had no part normally in the state rituals. We must not be misled by the English equivalents of the Indian words.

Under their colour were grouped a variety of lineages owing different services. We hear of carpenters, wheel-wrights, potters, smiths, fishermen, dog-leaders, and hunters.[3] There were drummers, conch-blowers and

[1] *Taitt. Br.* I, 1, 4, 8, acc. to MacDonell and Keith, II, 253.

[2] *Mhvs.*, XXX, 11.

[3] *Maitr. Samh.*, II, 9, 5.

flute-players.[1] There must have been barbers, in particular
a king's barber, to shave sacrificers after their consecration.
We know that some of these craftsmen held honourable
positions, since they are saluted ritually with the word
namas, which means "honour to." We shall see that
honour is still paid to them; we have seen that they held
important offices at court, so important that these posts
have since been taken over by royalty.[2] The term "serf"
evidently gives us no idea of their true position, for we
associate it with slavery; this we have come to look upon
as utterly degrading, though it is not necessarily so at all.
Prejudice completely blinds us to the fact that all depends
on the way slavery or serfdom is interpreted: slaves may
hold high office at court and even have the sovereign in
in their power. Serfs enjoy a somewhat higher status, as
they have privileges and honours fixed by ancient custom,
and of which they may be very tenacious. We must rid
ourselves of our prejudices concerning slavery and serfdom if we would understand the caste system in India or
elsewhere, and above all we must not confuse the serfs
with the outcastes. The so-called serfs are quite honourable
people who owe service to the king or feudal lord. We can
perhaps better describe them as retainers.

XIII

In books there is no need to explain how offices are
filled: it is usually common knowledge, and it is not usual
to write about matters of common knowledge. The ancient
writings are therefore silent on this point. We know that
to hold any office you had to belong to the right "colour,"
but we can only infer from modern custom that within
each "colour" there were houses which had the exclusive

[1] *Vaj. Samk.*, XXX, 5, 2, 2.
[2] Below, p. 103, and above, p. 20. *Kings and Councillors*, 178 *ff.*

right to certain offices; that not any serf, for instance, could be the king's charioteer, but only the members of a certain lineage. We have therefore to come down to present practice.

Unfortunately, my information on this point is only sufficient to point the way for further investigation.

It has been mentioned that the office of steward at the Temple of the Tooth is not open to all farmers, but only to two houses of farmer rank. It should further be noted that there is not a man appointed for life, but one man will come and officiate for a time and then go home, and another will take his place. In the same way, the drumming at the temple is not open to all drummers; it is in the hands of a house or houses, the members of which relieve one another and may hire assistance. It is easy to see how in this manner a caste may split up into subdivisions attached to different temples or lords, and which may draw apart to such an extent that they cease to intermarry.

These appointments, as we have said, are not paid, but certain lands are attached to them. This service tenure has been described by Knox in the eighteenth century: "In each of these towns there is a smith to make and mend the tools of them to whom the king hath granted them, and a Potter to fit them with Earthen Ware, and a Washer to wash their Cloathes, and other men to supply what there is need of. And each one of these hath a piece of Land for this their Service, whether it be to the King or the Lord; but what they do for other people they are paid for." This system still continues. I have visited a village of potters who supplied the neighbouring villages free in return for lands which they cultivated themselves. In the same way, the washerman holds land from the farmers he washes for. We can now perhaps understand why there is a farmer caste in a country where everyone farms: they are the landowners, and cultivation is their work in the State, and so in the ritual, for the State is a ritual organization; the others have other duties, and they cultivate only to feed themselves.

In addition to land the washermen receive certain perquisites: "the people give them paddy, eleusine; or, if they have none, money. . . . If any one dies in the village the washermen come with washed clothes provided by the people, and remove the clothes of the deceased. These clothes henceforth belong to the washerman. He is given to eat and drink and fifty cents for washing the clothes of the people who attend the funeral. The food is given on a leaf placed on a mat." I mention this detail because it is one of those acts of politeness towards the lower castes which I promised the reader.

In like manner, priests hold lands from the king.[1] They also receive fees which in Sanskrit are called *dakshina*. These are clearly not just commercial transactions such as take place between an English patient and his physician, or a litigant and his lawyer; they are offerings: for the priests, it should be remembered, represent the priestly gods.[2]

Priest, washerman and drummer are treated alike, for they are all priests; only the brahman is a higher kind of priest and so more munificently rewarded.

The high appointments in the State are made by the king; but his choice is limited by certain considerations, such as seniority. The first lie ever spoken was by a king who wanted to give the office of King's chaplain to the playmate of his youth. The chaplaincy was already held by this playmate's elder brother. The king could not override seniority, so he lied and declared the younger to

[1] Pope, *A Tamil Prose Reader*, 39.

[2] *Sat. Br.*, IX, 4, 1, 11; IV, 3, 4, 32; I, 9, 3, 1; XIV, 2, 2, 47; XIII, I, 1, 3.

be the elder.[1] On the other hand we hear of the son of a
brahman whose heredity office it was to consecrate the
state elephant; he did not know the necessary spells and
so was passed over.[2] It was not pure heredity, but heredity
tempered by fitness.

The farmers, too, appoint their retainers. If a village of
farmers find themselves without a washerman, they send
for one and settle him nearby to wash for them.

XIV

There are indications that these appointments were not
always as rigidly confined to the proper caste as they are
now supposed to be. In antiquity there appears to have
been a good deal of latitude. We hear of royalty becoming
priests. There was Janaka Videha, a supreme king, who
defeated the priests in argument, and asked of them as a
boon to receive the office of priest.[3] When Devapi was
dispossessed of his throne by his younger brother, he
asked to become the usurper's chaplain.[4] The *Harivamsa*
names two farmers who became priests.[5] Muir has
produced other cases.[6] There is a story that in a country
called Simhalakalpaya the royal family became extinct
and a merchant was placed on the throne.[7] In Ceylon in
the thirteenth century there was a movement to place a
man of farmer rank on the throne. The entry of the British
into Kandy was connected with a similar conspiracy.
Already the Rigveda knew of men "who falsely bear the
royal rank."[8]

These facts should remind us that Nature does not
obligingly fit into our social schemes, and that no system
can be rigid and survive. Some families die out, and their

---

[1] *Jataka*, III, 454.   [2] *Ibid.*, II, 163.   [3] *Sat. Br.*, XI, 6, 2, 10.
[4] *Nirukta*, II, 10.   [5] XI, 658.   [6] I, 229 *ff.*   [7] *Divyāvadana*, p. 523 *ff.*
[8] *Ep. Z.*, II, 64. *Rgv.*, VII, 104, 3.

places have to be filled; others multiply unduly, and so cannot all be placed. A barber with twelve sons cannot find them all a barbership. On the other hand, the whole community cannot remain in a state of pollution because all the available washermen have been wiped out by plague or by infertility. Then ambition and violence play havoc with constitutional theories. There are kings who have risen from the fourth caste. Energetic families seek to better their status. So common is it to rise in the scale that a Tamil proverb says a man of the thief caste may become a Maravan, by respectability an Agamudaiyan, and by slow degrees a farmer.[1]

I came across a community of washermen in the process of rising. In the south of Ceylon I visited a village of people who claimed to be descended from a prince, the son of King Gaja Bahu I, who renounced the throne for a washer-girl. They insisted they were not washermen, and did not wash, but had imported washermen to serve them; they bore names proper to the farmer caste, and styled themselves "village folk" (*gamagollan*), a term suggestive of a farmer. The headman, however, assured me behind their backs that they were washermen pure and simple.

Even the brahmans have failed to keep out aboriginal blood, as can readily be seen by the black skin and thick lips and noses of some of the southern ones.[2] In fact entry into their ranks was made easy by one school of thought which maintained that a brahman's "sanctity exempts him from any close inquiry into his real claim" to be a brahman.[3]

---

[1] Thurston, I, 7.

[2] E.g. Thurston, plate facing I, 341.

[3] MacDonell and Keith, II, 82, quoting *Pancavimsa Br.*, VI, 5, 8.

XV

As in every society lineages move down as well as up. Since rank depends upon certain qualifications, a family can lose its rank by losing its qualifications, or, as we have come to express it, "they lose caste."

One qualification is the strict observance of rules which go with certain offices. Since the offices are ritual the rules are ritual. We have already noticed one broad rule: that the sacrificer must eschew anything connected with death.[1] Hence a brahman may not officiate at a cremation or indeed be exposed to the smoke from a pyre.[2] A menstruating woman is also to be avoided, because, comparative evidence teaches us, the menstrual blood is death-dealing.[3] Each caste has its own rules which cannot at present be reduced to any common principle; but the attempt has never been made, and it is useless to make it, except comparatively.

Numerous are the castes which trace their present status to some departure from the rules of their caste. We should probably describe their fortunes more accurately by saying there are numerous families that have ceased to be qualified for certain functions, because they have broken the rules which qualified them. Such a breach results in a curse. Thus a son of Manu is cursed for having killed his teacher's cow, and so is reduced to the status of a serf.[4] The Mārakas of Mysore claim to be brahmans who were cursed by their teacher (that is, the head of the caste) as unfit to associate with the six sects of brahmans. There is a class of brahmans in the Tanjore district called "midday Pariahs," because an offended god cursed them to be Pariahs from noon till one daily.[5] Here the loss of status is only temporary. In extreme cases a family may be cast

[1] Above, p. 11. [2] *Manu*, IV, 69 [3] *Progress of Man*, 152.
[4] *Harivamsa*, XI, 659. [5] Thurston, I, 345 *f*.

out of the ritual organization altogether, so that they may not even take an external part in the ritual as do the serfs. Knox relates that the Roḍiyas of Ceylon were originally hunters, but one day, "instead of Venison they brought Man's flesh, unknown; which the King liking so well commanded to bring him more of the same Venison. The King's Barber chanced to know what flesh it was and discovered it to him." The king cursed them, and degraded them to their present vile status, "so base and odious, as not possibly to be more."[1]

Such stories are so common,[2] that we cannot possibly ignore them, and, consistently with the principle we have followed throughout, we must assume that the common gist of these stories is true, until we have definitely proved them to be wrong. We can only conclude then that the king as head of the state has the power to curse, and so degrade. The chieftains and the heads of the various lineages have the same power within their own jurisdiction. It is an extreme and permanent form of excommunication.

If we end where we should have started, with the observation of living societies, we may see excommunication at work. A case occurred in 1927 in the North-central Province of Ceylon. For details I am indebted to the Government Agent, Mr. M. M. Wedderburn. A certain man had married a woman who was an agnate of the same generation, and so of a prohibited degree.[3] They were reported to the headman, who sent his scribe to investigate. They were contumacious, so the headman interdicted the washermen from washing for that village. Now Sinhalese society cannot carry on without washerman or

[1] Knox, 70, 114. Cp. the Oriyas, Thurston, I, 175.

[2] Cp. *Ramayana*, I, 58, 7 (Muir, I, 402).

[3] The relationship is called *sahōdarī*. See Hocart, *Kinship Systems*, *Anthropos*, 1937, "The Indo-European Kinship System," *C.J.Sc.*, *G*, I, 183.

barber, not because they do not know how to wash or
shave, but because they can no more be born, married, or
die properly without washerman or barber than a Roman
Catholic can without a priest. That interdict brought the
offenders to heel; they paid a fine of which the headman
took one-third, the secretary another third, while the rest
went to make a feast at which the offenders ate with the
other people of their caste. This ceremonial eating together reinstated them.

Certain bangle-makers in South India keep a special
official whose duty it is to join in the first meal taken on
reinstatement by those who have been excommunicated.[1]

An Englishman's downfall may begin with "conduct
unbecoming an officer and a gentleman"; the king
cashiers him—that is, deprives him of his Army rank and,
by consequence, of his social status; he casts him out of
the society to which he had been born. Mere inefficiency
leads only to resignation or retirement, but it may lead
ultimately to the same result. It can be so in India too,
as witness certain South Indian weavers: the kings of
Madura were not satisfied with their workmanship and so
sent for foreign weavers from the north.[2]

XVI

Degrade a lineage and you leave a vacancy which has to
be filled, for the work of a brahman, or a barber, or a
washerman is necessary to the spiritual welfare of the
people. The way in which vacancies are filled is illustrated
by a story current in South India. Parasu Rama quarrelled
with some Brahmans, and procured himself new ones by
taking the nets of some fishermen and making out of them
brahminical threads with which he invested the fishermen,
and so turned them into brahmans. Later he cursed them

[1] Thurston, III, 288.   [2] *Ibid.*, 31.

E

for slighting him and returned them to the condition of
Śudras.[1]

Another South Indian story illustrates the king's
prerogative. A barber one day shaved the king without
waking him. The king was so pleased that he offered him a
boon. The barber asked to be made a brahman. The king
ordered the brahmans to make him one within six days,
on pain of forfeiting all their grants of lands. The barber
was to have a meal with them. In dismay, the brahmans
applied to the jester for help. He so turned the idea into
ridicule that the king desisted.[2]

Whether the story relates a true incident or not does
not concern us. We are not here trying to establish in-
cidents, but customs. Fiction is good evidence of custom,
because it tells us how people think things ought to
happen. It is well to check it with evidence, to make sure
it does not reflect idealism rather than fact; but here we
have other evidence that the king can alter status, and that
admission to a new status is clenched by a meal with those
who already are in it. The point of this story is that the
king's prerogative is never disputed, but only the fitness
of the barber for priestly rank. It is as if our king proposed
to confer a dukedom on a hairdresser, merely because
of his hairdressing. The prerogative would not be denied
but only the wisdom of its application.

We have numerous instances of kings fixing the
privileges of caste in South India. An inscription of the
eleventh century authorizes artificers to blow conches and
beat drums at their weddings and funerals, wear sandals,
and plaster their houses. In North Travancore many
families are in posession of royal edicts conferring upon
them the title of *Panikkar* (master), and along with it the
headmanship of the village in which they reside.[3] Such a

[1] Thurston, I, 373 *f.*   [2] Pope's *Tamil Prose Reader*, Story XXV.
[3] Thurston, III, 116; I, 41.

privilege at once marks off one family from another, and so produces a new caste.

The Sinhalese villagers who described for us the functions of drummers say it was the mythical King Mahasammata who decreed that only certain persons were to carry out the demon ceremonies. They evidently regard the king as the assigner of duties, the elector of functionaries.

The king himself had to be appointed. Mahasammata was elected, and so was Manu.[1] Comparative evidence assures us that election from within a certain lineage is more primitive than a rigid succession.

The election of the king and the appointment of officers naturally go together, since the king is the fount of office. This is especially the case when migration and conquest are active. Newcomers have to organize; they have to set up a king, and the king has to make himself a court. Situations such as arose out of the Norman Conquest, or our own expansion in India, are not uncommon at such times. A Chinese author tells us how a conqueror of Ceylon killed a merchant chief who came to the island in quest of gems, and "thus he extended his race. His sons and grandsons becoming numerous, they proceeded to elect a king and ministers and to divide the people into classes."[2] That does not mean that an entirely new social system was created (such a thing never happens), but simply that an existing pattern of society was adapted to new conditions by filling up the blanks.

We may from genealogies gain some idea of the principles which guided a king or his advisers in this task of filling vacancies. Take, for instance, that of the children of Manu: Some of his sons become *kshatriyas*.

[1] *Digha*, III, 93 f. J. Kautilya, *Arthasastra*, I, c. 13.

[2] S. Beal, *Si-Yu-Ki, Buddhist Records of the Western World* (Trubner's Oriental Series, 1884), II, 239 f.

Among the number is Ikshvaku, whom many a line of
kings claims as progenitor, notably the later kings of
Ceylon. Since he is first in the list, he is presumably the
eldest. Others became farmers. The last-named and
presumably the youngest, joined the fourth caste,
because, as we have related, he killed his preceptor's
cow. The descendants of some of his sons turned priests,
so that his descendants are distributed among all four
castes.[1] The process is repeated in a later generation.
From Śunaka issued the Śaunaka line, which includes
members of all four castes. The sons of Gritsamati were
priests, nobles, and farmers.[2] Here again ancient books
are confirmed by popular tradition: the South Indians
believe that the three castes of Maravan, Kallan, and
Agamudaiyan are descendants of three brothers. A caste
of village watchmen in South India trace their descent
to a man of the hunter caste.[3]

It is fashionable to reject such traditions as having
been forged to explain customs or for political purposes.
But forgeries to be convincing must be plausible; they
must agree with practice. You will not persuade people
that three castes are descended from three brothers, unless
it is considered well within the bounds of possibility.
Besides, what reasons have we to brand these genealogies
as forgeries except that we are obsessed by the doctrine
that aristocracy is based on conquest, or that caste is
based on technical specialization? We suffer also from an
automatic scepticism towards all ancient traditions.

We must leave our minds open for the possibility
that some of these traditions belong to a time when castes
were very elastic, and when the distances that separated
one from the other were much smaller than they are now:
for we know that inequality between classes tends to
increase. The ancient texts preserve memories of that lost

[1] Muir, I, 220 ff.   [2] Ibid., 227.   [3] Thurston, L, I, 26.

elasticity. They tell us that the second or third descendant of a nobleman (*kshatriya*) could become a member of the other three castes if he happened to eat the wrong food in lieu of *soma*.[1] That case is paralleled by that of a brahman who infused the warlike qualities of the nobility into a porridge; his daughter, as a result of eating it, bore a son half priest, half nobleman, while her mother by eating of a porridge differently prepared bore a full brahman.

All these texts refer to a bygone state of affairs, and we can hardly expect to support them with modern Indian practice, seeing this has changed so much. As usual, the conflict between ancient texts and modern scholars can only be settled by comparative evidence. It is not until we turn to a living society which preserves a caste system more archaic than even the ancient Indian that the text will be vindicated and understood. When we there see sons of the ruling house deputed to take charge of the various castes and to become members and chieftains of them, then we shall find it possible to believe and understand pedigrees such as those of Manu and Śunaka: they are not the pedigrees of the caste, but of cadets deputed from the royal house to lead the castes. The final battle will have to be fought outside India.

In the meantime, we can point out that language bears out traditions. The Sanskrit word *jyeṣṭha* means both higher in rank and eldest; *avarajā*, literally "low-born," means also younger brother; and the fourth caste is said to be junior (*yavīyas*) to the other three. In Ceylon the lower division of a caste is said to be *bāla*, young. Certain South Indian castes are addressed by terms of relationship—for instance, the members of various Telugu castes are addressed as *appa*, father; *amma*, elder brother, is a title of numerous other castes.[2] One subdivision of the pariahs is called *ammā*, mother.[3] In Ceylon a washerman

---

[1] *Ait. Br.*, VII, 29.   [2] Thurston, I, 48.   [3] *Ibid.*, 44.

is called "uncle *pedi*" and his wife "aunt *pedi*." The name of the Moplahs, who made themselves famous by their rebellion, means really "son-in-law." The Ceylon Moormen are addressed as *tambi*, younger brother; there is an Oriya caste which claims to be noble (*kshatriya*): the members call themselves *bhagipuo*, brother's sons, a term applied to a rajah's or a rajah's brother's illegitimate offspring. We can only conclude that they are descendants of a king's bastards, just as our Sinhalese "village folk" claimed to be.[1]

Popular opinion is evidently firmly convinced that there is a certain relationship between castes, and this can only be explained if we suppose that the founder of the caste, or some person deputed to lead the caste, stood in a certain relationship to members of another caste; that he was son, younger brother, nephew, or bastard, to the chieftain of the parent caste. There are bastard branches in India just as there are in England, and, as we shall find, in Fiji. Thus the Tamil oilmongers recognize a bastard branch called "son" or "child caste," which is parasitic on the true caste members.[2]

In some cases the union of two castes leads to a third one. The Tamil followers of the five crafts, goldsmith, blacksmith, coppersmith, carpenters, and masons, say they are descended from a priest and a merchant woman. Some say the Tamil accountants are the issue of a farmer by a woman of the fourth caste.[3]

Evidently mixed unions are not uncommon. I have seen a brahman *prima donna* who was reputed to be kept by a tenor of merchant status. The liaison was quite public. In fact, such unions are common enough to necessitate rules as to the status of the children. Manu lays down that the offspring of a man of priestly status by a farmer woman

---

[1] Thurston, I, 230. See above, p. 46.
[2] Thurston, VII, 313.　　　[3] *Ibid.*, III, 113; 150.

ranks as *Ambastha*, and he gives a whole list of such crosses.[1] Much controversy has raged about the list. The best way of settling it is to go and see.

XVII

The Indian caste system is far from being ossified: castes still come into existence; but the system is certainly more rigid than it used to be. The existence of ceremonies of admission to the caste seem conclusive on that point.

If we knew nothing about our constitutional history or that of Europe, it would be quite safe to deduce from our Coronation ceremony that primogeniture was not always inevitable as it is now. Why have a Coronation ceremony if the eldest had always succeeded his father automatically, and had been king from the moment of his predecessor's death? The Coronation has ceased to make any difference, and had consequently been dispensed with by most European nations before the war; but it must once have decided whether a man was king or not. Our reasoning would be perfectly correct: there was a time when a king was not a king till he had been consecrated.[2]

The same reasoning can be applied to the initiation ceremony which every youth of the three aristocratic castes has to undergo when he arrives at the proper age. The son of a brahman is not really a brahman till he has been initiated into the caste of his father. In a good family he will be initiated as a matter of course, and so he is thought of as a brahman before he really is one, just as our king is thought of as a king before his coronation, though, strictly speaking, he should not be, and cannot wear the crown. Our Coronation ceremony however has travelled much farther on the road to survival than the Indian initiation. If it were omitted, it would make no

[1] X, 1 *ff.* [2] *Kings and Councillors*, 131 *ff.*

difference. If the Indian initiation is omitted, the brahmanic youth falls to the status of a *vratya*; at least it was so when and where Manu's laws were written.[1] A nobleman's, a priest's and a farmer's rank thus still depends not only on birth, but on initiation. Birth itself is inadequate, "because," we are told by an ancient text, "he, indeed, is truly born who is born of prayer, of the sacrifice," whereas his first birth is doubtful: he may really be the result of demons implanting seed in a woman,[2] and we have seen that the representatives of demons are the non-sacrificial lineages.[3] A mere man has to be reborn as an aristocrat. The candidate for initiation is the sacrificer, and "becoming an embryo he is born from that sacrifice."[4] He becomes one of the deities.[5]

The castes are born of the sacrifice. There is no such contradiction as Muir imagines between the texts which say the castes are born of the sacrifice and those which trace the descent of the various castes from Śunaka or some other ancestor. It is quite possible for the different sons of one royal personage to be enrolled under the different colours by going through the initiation ceremony appropriate to that colour. Each one is the son of Śunaka by a woman, but he is at the same time the son of the sacrifice which he has celebrated in order to become a new man, or rather to be enrolled among the deities, if he is joining one of the three aristocratic colours.

In short, these myths do not tell us the origin of the caste system, but the basis of it, and that is twofold: descent and sacrifice. Of the two, sacrifice is the essential one; descent is merely a qualification which may at times be dispensed with. Another way of putting it is that these myths do not record an event that took place in the distant past, but a process which was continually re-enacted, the

---

[1] *Manu*, II, 38; X, 20.   [2] *Sat. Br.*, III, 2, 1, 40.
[3] Above, p. 19.   [4] *Sat. Br.*, III, 2, 1, 11.   [5] *Ibid.*, I, 1, 10.

ennobling of the sons of noble houses.[1] For preference, each one is raised to the rank of his father, but not inevitably. One ancient priest is recorded to have said, "If this rite of mine were complete, my own descendants would become noble, become priests, become farmers of the Salva tribe." Nothing could make it clearer that all nobles are not of one stock nor all priests of one stock, nor all farmers; but each tribe may fill these ranks from its own numbers by initiation. Just as bees are made into queens or workers by varying the diet, so kings' sons or priests' can become royal, priestly or farming by varying the ritual. It was believed that a king, according as he drank *soma*, curds or water (ritually, of course), would beget a son with the character of a priest, a farmer or a serf, whose descendants in the second or third generation become priests, farmers or serfs, as the case might be.[2]

If admission to royal, priestly or farmer rank is a rebirth, we should expect expulsion to be death. In fact, when a man has "fallen," "a female slave should overturn with the foot a full pot of water as for a dead man."[3]

XVIII

We are going very much beyond Indian evidence when we suggest that originally the initiation to a caste was limited to the head of the house; in other words, the initiation ceremony was originally a ceremony of installing the head of the caste. We are anticipating the evidence of other lands. Yet, speculative as it may seem, this suggestion must be mentioned here because there is evidence to

[1] Cp. my "Life-giving Myth" in *The Labyrinth*, ed. S. H. Hooke (London, 1934).

[2] *Ait. Br.*, VII, 29. Cp. *Vishnu Purana*, IV, 7, 14.

[3] *Manu*, XI, 184. Cp. "Medieval Outlawry and Excommunication," *Kings and Councillors*, 170 *f.*

be found in India that the trappings of headmanship have passed to the rank and file.

Before we deal with this evidence, we must clear away an assertion sometimes made that in Vedic times the castes were not organized under headmen. It is an argument from silence, and such an argument is worthless when we are dealing with ancient texts. The better known a fact is the less likely it is to be mentioned. Books are not written to proclaim what everybody knows, but to impart the unknown. Matters of common knowledge therefore only appear incidentally.

As a matter of fact, are the texts as silent as we imagine? They probably introduce us to a great many heads of castes without our knowing it. When we introduce Lord X, we do not always add, "He is the head of the house of Y," because that is well known or irrelevant. We can hardly expect our texts, every time they mention the king's courier, to notify us that he is the head of the courier caste, or of the house which holds the office of king's courier. If everyone knows that the army leader is the head of the house (colour black) to which that office belongs, why say so? Ultimately this point can only be settled by the study of living societies.

At the present day, castes in India have headmen. In Ceylon this must not be taken to mean that there is a chief washerman who is head of all the washermen throughout the length and breadth of the land; but that the various washermen's communities scattered all over the island have each its own head.

The chief man of a village of drummers is called a *panikkiyā*, or *vel-panikkiyā*. The headman of a *vahuṇpura* village is a *devayā*.[1] Several castes call their headmen *duraya*.[2]

---

[1] God? The people do not connect it with *deva*, god, which always appears in the plural form with singular meaning, *deviyo*.

[2] Skt. *dhura*.

To the farmer caste are reserved the titles *hāmi*, Lord, and *rāḷa*.[1] The latter formerly meant king, but has declined to little more than master.

In India it often happens that scattered groups belonging to a caste have a common headman. There is nothing in this inconsistent with what has been said: there is no reason why a house which increases and multiplies should not scatter, and still acknowledge a common head. Secondly, the term *jāti*, which we have unfortunately rendered "caste," is very elastic, as we saw, and may mean any sort of common descent. A whole tribe is a *jāti*, and when it is incorporated into Hindu society it remains a *jāti* with its own cult and customs. Since it is the cult and customs which are the main basis of caste, anyone starting a new cult with its new observances becomes detached from his lineage. For "caste is born of the ritual."[2]

After these preliminaries we can now come to the point. There is a tendency for headmen's titles to spread to the whole caste. Thus the title *Bindhani*, which is conferred on a member of a carpenter caste in South India, is sometimes applied to the whole caste. South Indian bankers and merchants are now commonly known as Chettis,[3] but in Sanskrit it means "the most distinguished," "the chief," and used to designate the head of a merchant house. Among the Kaikolan weavers of Mysore it remains the title of a headman.[4] The oilmongers of South India also style themselves Chetti.[5] The title of a headman in one place may be the name of a caste in another. Such is the Sinhalese *panikkiyā*, which means both a drummer chief and a barber.[6] The Sanskrit *adhikarin*, official,

---

[1] Skt. *svāmin* and *rājan*. *Temple of the Tooth*, 11.
[2] Thurston, I, 176; 220; 232; 125; etc.
[3] *Ceṭṭi*; Skt. *sreṣṭhin*.
[4] *Mysore Tribes and Castes*, III, 129.
[5] Thurston, I, 27; III, 13.
[6] *Temple of the Tooth*, 13 n.

means in Ceylon a minister; in South Canara a subdivision of a certain caste.[1] There is a Sinhalese caste called *durayā*; this term is the title of a headman in three other low castes.

This is the origin of some of the respectful terms used in addressing members of certain castes. We have seen that a Sinhalese washerman is politely addressed as "uncle chief washerman";[2] or else he may be called *henayā*, another headman's title which Mr. Paranavitana traces to Sanskrit *śreṇi*, head of a guild. The Tamils of Ceylon do not call a barber "barber" in his presence, but "farmer," unless they are angry with him. Even the utterly despised Rodiyas are not addressed by that name, but as Gaḍiya, Maṇḍukārayā, or Gasmanda, respectful terms.[3]

To such a point is this carried in Ceylon that headmen's titles are used as names. In fact, it may be said that among the Kandyan Sinhalese there are no proper names, but only titles. Almost every Kandyan farmer is called *Baṇḍā*, prince. A family may consist of nothing but princes, distinguished according to seniority, or colour, or affection, as Big Prince, Middle Prince, Small Prince, Little Prince, Black Prince, Milk Prince, Gold Prince.[4] Among farmers of low degree names formed from *rāla*, chief, are not uncommon; there are Small Chiefs, Milk

[1] Thurston, I, 3; VI, 404.

[2] Above, p. 54.

[3] It is not the business of the sociologist to pass judgment, but to observe the social structure and its working, and to explain these. Since, however, this objective is crossed by much bias, he has sometimes to remove that bias by pointing out the good side. I therefore underline the facts which show that the caste system is not all made up of contempt and oppression. It is a system in which each holds his little niche, and has his privileges and due honour. His disabilities are not thrown in his face unless he has asked for trouble.

[4] *Loku Baṇḍā, Māda Baṇḍā, Puñci Baṇḍā, Dingiri Baṇḍā, Kalu Baṇḍā, Kiri Baṇḍā*, etc.

Chiefs, etc.[1] Other names are compounded with *hāmi*,
lord. None of these names can be given to persons of
low degree. The daughters of Big House are "jewels,"
great or small. The lower orders use the titles peculiar to
them. The washerman title of *henayā*, for instance, is
often incorporated in the personal name, if indeed personal
names can be said to exist.[2] I have a list of names of the
smith caste:[3] half the men are called *nayidē*, which is a
respectful term to an artificer; all the women are *naccirē*,
which is the feminine equivalent. They are distinguished
from one another as big, little, milk. There are four potters
in my list, all likewise called *nayidē*, but the adjectives are
different from those of the smiths. So fine is the line
between proper names and titles that a Kandyan lady told
me that all Low Country washermen were called Fer-
nando.[4]

In Ceylon the name of the house precedes that of the
individual: it constantly refers to a title-holder. To give
an instance, a smith in my list prefixes to his name "of the
house of the coronet-bearing chiefs Vijendra."[5] A potter
calls himself "Glory-increasing artificer of the house of
the master of arts by the king's favour."[6] This last is an
example of how the king is the fount of honour.

This extension of titles from the chief to the common

[1] *Puñcirāla, Ukkurāla.*

[2] If anyone were to suggest that personal names are derived from
titles, he would be laughed at. Yet here is a country of no mean civilization
where people are content to call their children by titles, and nothing else.
Why should people have personal names at all? It is convenient, but
convenience does not necessarily bring a custom into existence, or we might
have had the telephone in prehistoric times.

[3] *Navandana.*

[4] Portuguese names are common in the Low Country. Here is a good
instance how little foreign influence affects the *mould* of a society, however
much it may alter the *contents*.

[5] *Vijendrapatabandi muhandiramalage.*

[6] *Rajakaruna Paṇḍita yalä Sirivāḍi Nayidē.*

crowd can be traced at least as far back as Buddhist literature. Not only the king, but members of the royal caste are there called rajahs. A peasant is addressed as "head of the house"; in fact, the plural "heads of houses" is synonymous with "men of farmer descent."[1]

Another way of designating the members of a caste is by describing them as sons of the title-holder. In the ritual books we find the expression "king's sons," only it is restricted to real sons of kings, as opposed to *rajanya*, "the royals," who are the inferior members of royal lines. In the form *Rajput* the title "king's son" now seems to cover the whole caste. We also find such terms as "son of a priest," "son of a merchant."[2] The "son of a smith" is not necessarily a young smith, but one who is not the head of the family.[3] In the same way, the son of a king is called a "royal youth," or simply "youth," whatever his age.[4] The Prince of Wales was in Ceylon known as "The Youth," and was called so until he became king. In the Sinhalese language princes are called "royal boys."

Thus words meaning "young" have curiously enough come to be honorific terms, so that in Ceylon you address a highly respected person as *hāmuduruvo*, which originally meant "lord's children" or "noble children."[5] The Tamils use their word for "child" as an honorific which is attached

---

[1] *Jataka*, I, 352. *Digha*, II, 145: *khattiyaparisā, brahamaṇaparisā, gahapatiparisā*.

[2] *Sat. Br.*, XIII, 5, 2, 10. *Jataka*, III, 475. *Rgv.*, II, 43, 2: *Brahmaputra*.

[3] *Digha*, II, 126.

[4] *Rājakumāra, kumāra, Jataka*, III, 122, 475.

[5] Skt. *svamin+dahara*. Professor W. Geiger was puzzled by the term "boy" applied in *Mhvs.*, XXXVII, 100 to the brother of a king of Ceylon who had reigned twenty-seven years. My friend therefore resorted to an emendation which is contradicted by the Rajavaliya and inscriptions. See Geiger's *Culavamsa*, I, 17. This illustrates the advantages of the comparative method. Such a passage would have no difficulty for one who knows that elderly men of rank are called "boys" in Ceylon, Fiji, Tonga, and elsewhere. Below, pp. 109, 110, 117, 120.

to names of the farmer caste.[1] The members of a
South Indian village assembly are called "the great
children."[2]

We may suggest as a possible explanation that it
designates the near relations of the heads of castes, as
opposed to the inferior branches that are not in the
running for the headship. Hence it means a person of
the highest status within the caste.

Thus we have evidence that the honours due to a chief
have spread to his subjects until his title has become a
name used by any member of the family or caste. Our
suggestion that the initiation ceremony has had a similar
history becomes quite a reasonable one. It would be considerably strengthened if we could find living societies
where there is no ceremony of admission to the caste,
but only an installation of the head of it, and if initiation
and installation both followed somewhat the same lines.
The obvious way is to look round for such a society.[3]

XIX

Before we go in search of one, it is well to notice another
classification of lineages besides that into four colours.

In South India they classify them into two divisions,
right and left. Unfortunately, little is known about this
arrangement, because it is not mentioned in texts: it is
not classical. Yet it is so important for comparative
purposes that we must put together whatever fragments
have come to our notice.[4]

---

[1] *Pillai*; honorific plural, *pillaiyar*. Thurston (*s.v.*) says: "Many Pariah
butlers of Europeans have now assumed the title *pillai* as honorific suffixes
to their names."

[2] *Perumakkal*. H. Krishnasastri, "Fiscal Administration," in *Bhan-
darkar Commemoration Volume*, 227.

[3] Below, p. 110.

[4] For its comparative importance, see *Kings and Councillors*, XX.

J. A. Dubois[1] says:

"Most castes belong either to the Left-hand or Right-hand faction. The former comprises the Vaisyas or trading classes, the Panchalas[2] or artisan classes, and some of the Sudra castes. It also contains the lowest caste—namely, the Chucklers,[3] or leather-workers, who are looked upon as its chief support.

"To the Right-hand faction belong most of the higher castes of Sudras. The Pariahs are its chief support, as a proof of which they glory in the title of Valangai-mongattar,[4] or friends of the Right-hand. In the disputes and conflicts which so often take place between the two factions it is always the Pariahs who make the most disturbance and do the most damage.

"The Brahmins, Rajahs, and several classes of Sudras are content to remain neutral. . . .

"The rights and privileges for which the Hindus are ready to fight such sanguinary battles appear ridiculous to a European. Perhaps the sole cause of the contest is the right to wear slippers or to ride through the streets in a palanquin or on horseback during marriage festivals."

Thurston supplies a concrete example of these disputes. The Beri merchants are a leading left-hand caste. They are not allowed to tie plantain trees to the posts of the wedding arches so that they touch the ground, as other people do. If they transgress this rule, the Pariahs cut them down.[5]

[1] *Hindu Manners and Customs* (Oxford, 1897), I, 25.

[2] I.e. the five crafts.

[3] Tamil *šakkili.*

[4] *Valangaimugattār* (vulgo, *valangamattār*).

[5] I, 213; cp. III, 327. Such facts again lend a very different complexion to the Indian caste system from the orthodox—I might say, official—view. The humblest have their privileges which they can enforce against their betters, and the highest have their disabilities. The system has been judged by the theory, and the theory is very different from the practice. The brahmans who put forth such arrogant claims in *The Laws of Manu* and

Unfortunately, Dubois never localized his evidence, but gave us a general impression, a composite picture of several varieties of the same system. Such a composite picture is useful as an introduction, but is as dangerous to work with as an imaginary crustacean made up of parts taken from the crab, the hermit crab and the lobster.

It is evident that this dualism assumes different forms in different parts of India, and we shall not make much progress as long as we pick here and there. The only way to get the system as a whole is to study definite communities exhaustively, even as we do with species.

For instance, Dubois tells us that the castes are ranged into two factions. That may be right for one area, but we learn that in some parts there are barbers on both sides.[1] The Mala outcastes are similarly distributed.[2] Both the right and the left are represented in a Malayalam caste of weavers, the left-hand being considered superior. A caste is not always on the same side everywhere: some Conjeevaram weavers belong to the right, others to the left.[3]

Mr. Sivajnanam, whose mother is of Travancore, tells me that in her country the farmers are divided into those who tie the end of the cloth on the right and those who tie it on the left. The two parties may intermarry. He thinks the left-hand people are descendants in the female line, and supports his opinion with the fact that if breath be taken through the right nostril at conception the child will be male; if through the left, female.

other works were probably finding compensation for the fact that they were entirely in the hands of their inferiors. In the East the lowest have developed the art of self-protection to a pitch unrealized in Europe, where it is not yet as necessary in order to survive. Knox has described how even the Rodiya outcastes used to turn their very untouchability into a kind of blackmail to extort alms.

[1] Thurston, I, 213.

[2] S. Nicholson, "Social Organization of the Mala," *J.R.A.I.*, 1926, 91.

[3] Thurston, VI, 361; II, 11.

F

Those who have made a comparative study of the social structure, and are aware of the so-called dual organization, will at once realize the importance of Mr. Sivajnanam's evidence. In the dual organization the two groups are male and female lines, and intermarry.

There is yet a further variation which points the same way. In the Madura region, while the men among the leather-makers "belong to the right-hand faction, the women belong to and are most energetic supporters of the left. It is even said that during the entire period of a faction riot the Chakkili women keep aloof from their husbands and deny them their marital rights."[1] This again suggests that originally right and left intermarried. We need concrete cases of Chakkili marriages to get at the bottom of this question.

There is a South Indian legend of the origin of this dual system which is worth recording because it once more shows the king as head of the caste, and shows how fundamental is the rivalry of the two groups, another characteristic of the dual organization.

The legend relates that the farmers claimed the artisans as their caste dependants, and the artisans claimed the farmers. "The fight grew so fierce that the Chola king of Conjeevaram ranged these two castes and their followers on opposite sides and enquired into their claims. The artisans and those who sided with them stood on the left of the king, and the farmers and their allies on the right. The king is said to have decided the case against the artisans." Of course, this legend, as is usual with legends, does not give us the origin of the system, but only an award in one of the quarrels that are a necessary part of it.

[1] *Manual of the Madura District*, quoted by Thurston, II, 4.

XX

What relation does this twofold system bear to the fourfold? The comparative student will have no difficulty in deciding that the twofold is an earlier one that has been overlaid, and sometimes superseded, by the fourfold. The distribution of these two systems seems decisive by itself; but let us see what evidence we can pick up on Indian soil.

1. The fourfold system alone is mentioned in the ancient books of the north and those southern books that represent the infiltration of the northern caste system.

2. The twofold division is evidently decaying in the south. It has all the appearance of a survival, and it is not easy to get more than scraps of information. The Tamils of India have it, but those of Ceylon have lost it and speak in terms of the fourfold system, as do the Sinhalese. There are, however, in Ceylon traces of the dual organization, notably the kinship system.[1]

3. Different forms of the right and left divisions are found in Burma, Siam and Cambodia, which fits in with the theory that the fourfold system came from the north-west and spread southwards and eastwards.[2]

XXI

In conclusion, the Church and the State are one in India. The head of this Church-State is the king. He is the head of the ritual, but he does not carry it out alone; in fact, most of the actions and words belong to his vassals, who would be described as King's serjeants if they

[1] My "Indo-European Kinship System," *C.J.Sc.*, G, I, 205; I, 181 *ff.* Hocart, "Buddha and Devadatta," *Indian Antiquary*, LIV (1925), 98. H. G. Quaritch Wales, *Ancient Siamese Government* (London, 1934).

[2] *C.J.Sc.*, G, I, 208 *ff. Rep. A.S.I.* (1902-3), 95.

were English. These officers are not appointed at random, but from specified families, unless these fail by extinction, or incapacity, or sin. The man who shaves the king, as required by the ritual, is appointed from a family which takes its rank from its head, a low rank, since the office of barber is low, being polluting. The great master of ritual we call a priest, and he is so high that he becomes higher than the king, so his line ranks above all others, farmers, artisans and the rest. Thus lineages are classified according to the office they are entitled to.

The king's state is reproduced in miniature by his vassals: a farmer has his court, consisting of the personages most essential to the ritual, and so present even in the smallest community, the barber, the washerman, the drummers and so forth.

The temple and the palace are indistinguishable, for the king represents the gods. Therefore there is only one word in Sinhalese and in Tamil for both.[1] The god in his temple has his court like the king in his palace: smiths, carpenters, potters, all work for him.

This ritual organization has spread downward to such an extent that the poor cultivators in the jungle have their retainers to play the part which they alone are qualified by heredity to play at births, weddings, and funerals, but these retainers are retainers of the community, the village, not of one lord.

A social system is always unique when taken in all its details, but never in its broad lines. There is no social organization exactly like that of Ceylon, or of Madura, or of Benares in every point; but there are systems which are like them in their general structure, because they have diverged from a common parent organization. By studying these we shall increase our understanding of Indian facts, because they often preserve earlier forms.

[1] S. *māligāva;* T. *Maligai.*

Persia

ANCIENT Persia is scarcely known outside a small circle of experts, modern Persia not at all. For one who is not an expert to venture into this unknown land may seem presumption indeed. But what are experts there for unless it is to guide the inexpert? If they are truly expert we are safe in sticking closely to their translations and commentaries; if we are not safe they cannot claim to be experts. I shall therefore trust implicitly J. Darmesteter's French translation of the *Zend-Avesta*.[1] If we go astray, the blame will be his.

I. Caste does not mean that a man must follow the occupation of his father. "La caste sacerdotale est trop nombreuse pour vivre tout entière de l'autel. En fait l'immense majorité des Mobeds[2] vit de professions laïques, principalement du commerce" (I, li). Here I will just observe that numbers are not the chief reason. Comparative evidence makes it clear that at no time did all the members of a caste officiate. But more of that hereafter.

II. There are four castes. "Quelles sont ces quatre classes?[3] Prêtre, guerrier, laboureur, artisan" (Hâ 19, v, 17; notes I, 169).[4]

How do those who disbelieve in the fourfold system of the Indian writers account for the same theory in Persia? Is that also no more than a figment of the priests? If so,

---

[1] "Le *Zend-Avesta*," *Annales du Musée Guimet* 21 (Paris, 1892).

[2] The equivalent of the Indian brahmans.

[3] Lit. occupation.

[4] Their ancient names are *āthravan* (later *mobed*), *rathaêshar*, *vastryo-fshuyâs*, *huitish*.

how did Indian and Persian come independently by the same idea? There must have been something very obviously pointing that way in the facts of both countries. The most natural conclusion is that this classification did not develop on Indian soil, but either in Persia from where it spread to India, or in a third region which gave it to both.

III. The first three castes stand apart. "Généralement l'Avesta ne cite que les trois premières classes. . . . De même les proclamations d'Ardashîr . . . s'adressent 'aux docteurs qui sont le soutien de la religion, aux cavaliers qui défendent l'état . . .; aux laboureurs qui donnent la fécondité.' "

The last words throw some light on the function of the third caste: in this system for securing prosperity, they make the soil fertile.

IV. The first three castes are sacrificial. Each has its own sacred fire. "La société avestéene connaît trois classes: prêtres, guerriers, laboureurs, et chacune de ces classes a un feu spécial qui veille sur elle." This sacred fire endows the priests with learning, the warriors with speed and bravery, the agriculturists with skill as cultivators. It is not specialization in skill then, but in the supernal grace received. Out of this develops specialization in skill.[1]

Each caste derives its qualities from its sacred fire (the Indian theologian would say they were born of the sacred fire). Each of these three castes has its own glory, but their glories are contained in the king's glory. There are three invocations, one for each fire. "Chacune de ces trois invocations se termine par celle de la gloire Royale ou du Hvarenô des Kavis, parce que le roi étant le patron des trois classes, sa Gloire est composée de la Gloire de

[1] *Kings and Councillors*, 30, 39, 285 ff.

ces trois classes:[1] aussi quant Yima,[2] aprés sa faute, est abandonné du Hvarenô, le Hvarenô s'enfuit de lui en trois fois" (I, 152 f.; *Yasht*, XIX, 34-8). We have seen that in India the king includes the gods of other castes and shall see that in Fiji too the divinities of the clans are included in the divinity of the king.[3]

V. The organization is sacrificial and therefore it is entered through the sacrifice. Birth is not sufficient; initiation is indispensable. "Un fils de Mobed n'est pas par cela même Mobed et n'a pas *ipso facto* le droit d'exercer. Il faut qu'il ait passé par un certain nombre de cérémonies initiatoires. Ces cérémonies sont au nombre de trois.... Par ces cérémonies il devient tour à tour Behdin, ... Herbed et Mobed."

"La première cérémonie.... n'est pas spéciale au Mobed: c'est une cérémonie par laquelle tous doivent passer: c'est l'initiation qui fait entrer l'enfant ... dans la communauté zoroastrienne; c'est la cérémonie qui fait de lui un Beh-dîn, c'est à dire un fidèle de la Bonne Religion" (I, li). Thus there is a common initiation into the aristocracy followed by special initiations into the branches of the aristocracy; just as we have B.As. followed by specialized doctorates.

VI. There is, as in India, a time limit for the initiation. "Il doit, pour dernier délai, le prendre à l'âge de quinze ans: faute de quoi il devient la proie des démons" (I, lii).[4]

VII. Though birth is not sufficient, it is essential.

---

[1] Cp. the Sinhalese consecration as described in the *Mahavamsa Tika*, Batuwantudawe's, ed. (Colombo, 1895) p. 213, where the king has to be baptized by a member of each of the three sacrificial castes. *Commentary on Mhvs.*, XI, 33. Comparative evidence shows this to mean that the "virtue" of the three castes is put into the king. Cp. *Kings and Councillors*, 93 *ff*.

[2] He committed incest with his sister. In India Yama is always entitled king, not god. *Progress of Man*, 208.

[3] Above, p. 37, and below, p. 85.

[4] Darmesteter refers to *Vendidad*, XVIII, 54-9.

All priests are supposed to be of one common stock. "Tous les prêtres de Perse, dit le Bundahish, forment une seule et même famille descendue du roi Mânûschihir."[1] Like the Brahmans, they are descendants of kings.

Within this family there is specialization. Thus the priests of Mansârî are divided into five families: No. 1 performs funeral ceremonies; No. 2 guards the Nîrang; No. 3 begins the prayer in the assembly of priests; No. 4 initiates the two higher grades; No. 5 keeps the Anjuman's register. Note that the funeral ceremonies, as usual, require a special staff. On the other hand the function of opening proceedings, which so often characterizes the priesthood, seems here to be the speciality of one branch, No. 3.[2]

Classes that owe their privileges to birth naturally insist upon birth, and would always make it a *sine qua non*, if Nature would let them, for a privilege ceases to be a privilege if it spreads too widely. Nature, however, does not respect birth as much as those who can boast of it. There is talent without and ineptitude within, and you cannot for ever keep one down and the other up. The most rigid rules of birth can be circumvented, and no doubt it was so in Persia as everywhere. There was as in India a school that laid stress on qualifications rather than on birth. "Je proclame Ratu[3] du prêtre celui qui connait le mieux la religion mazdéene" (I, 123; Hâ 12, vv. 2 f.).

VIII. There were people who missed their initiation and sank. They became "the prey of demons." Persia agrees with India in regarding the uninitiate as demoniac. In consecrating the communion bread the following words are used: "Et celui qui, parmi ces adorateurs de

---

[1] Cp. the genealogy on p. lvii.

[2] Above, p. 68; below, p. 90.

[3] =Skt. *rājan*, king, but as in India it has declined.

Mazda, étant en âge et capable de répéter, ne reçoit
pas, ne prononce pas ces paroles [après moi], celui-là est
convaincu d'être un Yatu" (I, 76). A *yatu* is a sorcerer, a
magician, a man who follows the religion of Ahriman.
The man who does not carry out the ritual duly is rejected
from among the godly, and becomes one of the demoniac,
just as in India "the assembly that does not hold soma
sacrifices" is an assembly of giants or demons, opponents
of the gods; just as with us sinners, non-communicants,
witches, and heathens are all enrolled under the devil's
banner. They can have no share in the sacrifice. "Qu'ils
s'enfuient d'ici! Que s'enfuient les Dâevas et les adorateurs des Dâevas" (Hâ 10, v. 1).[1] To offend against
Ahura Mazda is to lose caste, for it is inconsistent with
membership of the first three, or godly castes. "Si
quelqu'un me ravit, me dérobe, ou m'enlève la part que
m'a donné le saint Ahura Mazda . . . dans sa maison ne
naîtra ni prêtre, ni guerrier, ni laboureur" (P. 110 *ff.*,
Hâ 11, vv. 5 *f.*).

Thus the sins of the fathers are visited on his descendants, and the curse brings down the lineage.

---

[1] *Daeva* = Skt. *deva*, but means exactly the opposite, "giants"; while
ahura is the same etymologically as Skt. *asura*, but means "the good god."
For a possible explanation of this curious inversion, see *Kings and
Councillors*, 270.

Fiji

I

STUDENTS of culture are too much bounded by geography. For them Asia is Asia and the Pacific is the Pacific, and never may the twain be allowed to meet. Human nature, however, is not so bounded; it overleaps geographical limits; Asia overflows into Africa and the South Seas. Indonesia is but a continuation of it, and Polynesia a continuation of Indonesia.

If, like the brahmans, our students of culture fear to cross the sea, they will miss a social organization which resembles the Indian, not in general principles only, such as feudal and ritual character, but sometimes in such minute details as the honorific use of the word "child" to denote caste members. If it merely resembled India, the comparison would be curious, but would not advance our inquiries into the growth of social organization. It also differs, and the differences are mostly, not always, in the direction of greater archaism. In Fiji we get nearer to the parent system than in the oldest writings of India.

We have another advantage in Fiji, and that is that we need not be content with scraps or composite pictures. Several communities have been studied in great detail, and a great part of the remaining ones cursorily for purposes of comparison. They have not been fused into an ideal Fijian society, but each organization has been kept apart, so that every custom and office appears in its proper place in its proper system.

This is most necessary, as there are considerable variations in Fiji. There is some sort of caste all over Fiji, but it is among the tribes which I have called the

Koro Sea Tribes, because they ring round this sea, that it is most definite and well-developed.[1] It is that variety to which I shall mainly confine myself; but we shall find it necessary to go to other tribes to find more archaic forms, notably to central and northern Vanua Levu, which preserves an earlier substratum somewhat damaged and overlaid by invasions from Viti Levu.[2]

II

It is customary to divide Fiji into tribes, tribes into villages, and villages into clans, and thus we come to imagine Fiji somewhat on the analogy of our states sub-divided into provinces and districts. The reality is not so definite; it is not always easy to say where one tribe ends and another begins, because the foundation of Fijian society is not administration, but allegiance, and allegiance may vary infinitely from ritual subservience combined with political independence to complete serfdom. Fealty may be due to more than one suzerain; for to be a suzer-ain does not mean to give orders to the vassal about internal administration, but to receive offerings and service.

The whole of Fijian society is in fact based on offerings and service, and the exact nature of the suzerainty is discussed in terms of offerings and service: whether a noble lord is entitled to first fruits, to wading-ashore gifts, or only to a change of clothes, whether the border can be required to carry feasts for him or not, and so on.[3] The

[1] Hocart, "Ethnographical Sketch of Fiji," *Man*, 1915, 4.
[2] So far only one exhaustive study of a community has got into print. That community is Lakemba in the Windward Islands (Hocart, *Lau Islands*, Honolulu, 1929). The rest of the Koro Sea Tribes and the whole of Vanua Levu remain in manuscript. The Hill and Western tribes are still in the original notes, and so will hardly appear.
[3] *Lau*, 28 f., 75. Cp. *Kings and Councillors*, 104, 135.

offerings may be from equal to equal, as in the case of two equal intermarrying tribes, but even in equality there are degrees, for there is an unequal equality where one tribe ranks above another in virtue of a myth, though it may be inferior in power and prestige.[1]

To understand the nature of these offerings, we must remember that the Fijian chief stands for a god;[2] he is in fact more important than the gods, and may supersede them in the receipt of offerings. I know of two cases in which offerings to the gods were diverted from the gods: in one case to the suzerain, in the other to the sons of a lady imported from the suzerain state.[3]

Thus at the very outset we find the whole feudal system of Fiji resting on ritual.

In this rather vague and fluid system of allegiance it is possible to mark off certain territories as more compactly knit together. Fijians will discuss whether a certain community is "a face of the lord,"[4] an expression which we may render as "sovereign state." For instance, Lakemba and the islands to the south gravitate round the Lord of Nayau, and no other; they are recognized as a sovereign state, though they certainly owed some allegiance to Mbau. Within that group each island with its satellites forms a unit; but the most definite and self-contained unit is the village.

The village is subdivided into equally definite groups of twenty to thirty souls. I have so far called these groups clans for lack of a better term, but it is not a good one, since these units have nothing in common with Scottish clans. A clan acknowledges a common ancestor who may be no more than two generations removed from the oldest

---

[1] E.g. Vuna which ranks above Mbau, the greatest state of Fiji.

[2] *Kings and Councillors*, 61, 88.

[3] *Ibid.*, 104.

[4] *Mata ni tu:* the exact idea is difficult to get at, but *mata* means face, and *tu* chief, lord. We shall have more to say about the word "face."

member. Several clans may acknowledge a common ancestor: they are branches of the same lineage. The clan is based on descent, but it is also based on something more, as its very name shows.

The Fijian word is *matangali*. *Ngali* means vassal. *Mata* is more difficult: it means eye, face, front, presence. How do these meanings fit? Nothing less than an excursus on the word will answer that question. The word plays a great part in ritual. We hear of faces of the temple, faces of the grave. There is the tomb, and the top, the tumulus, is the face of it just as "the face of the water" is the place where the water comes to the surface, a spring. Hence *mata* alone comes to be used of a sacred place, a grave, and there are villages called *Na Mata*, the holy land. A *matangali* then is a holy land in a state of vassalage, whereas a *matanitū* is the tumulus of a sovereign lord.[1]

This interpretation is confirmed by the statement of the Lord of Tokatoka, who calls his clans *matambure*, faces, fronts of the temple instead of *matangali*. "The temple fronts," he says, "are our clans, the temples where the various gods are served. The tribes are different; they have a common descent; the temple fronts are different; they are smaller, they are groups of brothers and agnatic cousins[2] with their several temples." In short, a clan is a group of close relations who own a temple. The four noble clans of Lakemba were an apparent exception; they had only one temple between them, but they always insisted they were not clans, but only houses treated as clans for the purpose of assessments.[3] In Suva the term

---

[1] Lorimer Fison, by an over-ingenious argument, arrived at the meaning "group." Unfortunately, he did not take into account all the meanings of *mata*. I followed him in my *Lau Islands*, but after reviewing all the evidence I cannot find any trace of the idea of group, and I do not believe it is ever present to the Fijian mind. The reader will have to judge for himself when he has seen further evidence.

[2] *Veita* ✕ *ini*.   [3] *Lau*, 12.

"front of the temple"[1] means not a clan, but a subdivision of it. Just as there are heads of clans and a chief over them, so there are clan temples and a state temple[2] for the whole tribe. In fact, a tribe may be conceived as a temple. Thus in Ndravuwalu, in the island of Kandavu, the clans of the commons,[3] when bringing offerings, are headed by a chieftain whose title is Lord of the Sacred Land.[4] When they are all gathered together they are called "The Divine temple,"[5] because they own the god. Whole villages or states are sometimes named "State Temple."[6] In the same way clans are commonly called after the house of their head or after their temple.

The case of Ndravuwalu sums up the nature of the Fijian state: the people come together, they form a state, for the holding of feasts, of ceremonial exchanges, of the chief's or the god's corvée, not for the routine of life, such as digging, building ordinary houses, or communications. They come together as what we should call a Church, only our Churches are highly specialized, whereas in Fiji Church and State are even less differentiated than in India.

In these state feasts and ceremonials each clan brings its contribution. The clan is thus an assessment unit. Each cooks its quota and so is "an oven."[7] If a feast is decided upon the council does not assign the contributions per head, but per clan. Each clan, big or small, contributes the same amount. If a clan is very much depleted it finds it hard to raise its quota; if it has multiplied greatly it can take things too easily. Therefore excessively large clans are split up, and excessively small ones are fused with another that is closely related.[8] If we remember that feasts

---

[1] Here it is *mata ni mbure*. The exact shade of meaning conveyed by *ni*, of, is not clear.

[2] *Mbure ni Tu*, lit. "temple of the lord."

[3] *Lewe ni vanua.*   [4] *Tu ni Mata.*   [5] *Mbure kalou.*

[6] *Mburetu, Murenitu, Nasava*, etc.   [7] *Lovo.*   [8] *Lau,* 12.

are not just meals with guests, but offerings to the god or
the chief, we are brought back to our original proposition
that the whole organization of society in Fiji is based on
ritual: little Churches all come together at times to form
one big Church, which itself may pay tribute to a bigger
Church. The head of the Church is the head of the community.

III

Each clan has its status, "its standing,"[1] as the Fijians
put it; they belong to some caste, as we should say in
India.

Some are noble, some are low, but nobility and lowness
shade off into one another, and there is no sharp division
such as exists in India. That is typical of Fijian society
and thought: they have an elasticity which it is hard for us
to grasp, and it is impossible to translate them into our
terms without introducing a definiteness that is not in the
original.

One reason why we cannot draw a sharp line between
high and low is that no clans are excluded from the ritual.
That was only to be expected by those who knew that
the Fijians make no distinction of gods and giants, light
and dark, good and evil. Exclusion from the ritual is
therefore not Fijian; yet there is one exception: the caste
known as "King's Carpenters"[2] "did not attend or speak
in a gathering of chiefs." It must be remembered that
the chiefs only foregathered to discuss ritual,—that is to
say, feasts, ceremonial exchanges, chiefly births or
funerals, the building of temples or chiefs' houses, first-
fruits, visits of kindred chiefs,[3] anything connected with

---

[1] *I tutu.*   [2] *Mataisau.*

[3] The formal coming of guests, e.g. after a death, is a ritual occasion,
because they represent the gods. Hocart, "The Divinity of the Guest,"
C.J.Sc., G, I, 125.

the service of the king or the gods, not to plan new
roads, frame an educational policy, or regulate the hours
of work. The King's Carpenters were thus excluded from
the state ritual. No one would intermarry with them,
and, in Suva at least, no one would even eat of a pudding
prepared by them. They were not formed into clans in
Mbau, but were there distributed among the nobles.
The King's Carpenters, then, are an exception, but one
that proves the rule, for they are a late intrusion. They
say they drifted down in the Flood some five generations
ago from the north of Viti Levu, and were dispersed
among a few of the more important states, especially on
the Lower Rewa.[1] They are not an integral part of Fijian
society.

If we look for the grouping into colours, we shall find
it merely as a survival in Vanua Levu. I have already
described it as the division into Black Bodies and Red
Bodies.[2] It is a twofold and not a fourfold division, and
that is a characteristic difference between Fiji and
Northern India. Fiji is permeated with dualism, as South
India, and the greater part of the world, have once been.[3]
Fourfold divisions play a great part in Fiji, but more as
survivals than as living institutions.

IV

If we want to draw a line between Fijian castes, the most
marked division is perhaps between the king's or chief's
family and the rest of the people. This family is constantly
referred to as the *tūraña*; I shall call them the nobles, or
the nobility, or the royal caste.[4] The proper meaning of

---

[1] Mbau, Rewa, Suva, Naitasiri, Somosomo, etc.

[2] Above, p. 30.

[3] *Kings and Councillors*, XX.

[4] *Tūraña* seems to be compounded of *tū* plus an unknown word, *raṇa*.

the word *tūraña* seems to be chief, whether of a state, or village, or clan, but being used of all the members of the chief's family, it comes to mean king, aristocrat, gentleman, headman, even old man. Thus there may be clan chieftains who are *tūraña* in the sense of chief, but not in the sense of aristocrat, nobleman.

In the opinion of some the great nobilities of Fiji, including states once great, but now decayed, belong all of them to one single stock that came from Moala.[1] Another widespread legend traces them to Verata.

However that may be, there are degrees among them. The aristocracies of Mbau, ҳakaundrove and Rewa, towered above the others. They ennobled through their women many tribes that had no aristocracies, or only second-rate ones. In fact, there were states which, for the lack of blue blood among them, could have no king or chief, but were ruled by chieftains. The way out was to obtain the hand of a lady of noble blood for their own chief. Her offspring were recognized as noble, and indeed in Na Mata the sons of such a lady were given the best part of the offerings which had previously been given to the gods. Thus this stock, whether it came from Moala or Verata, played the same part as the solar and lunar dynasties in India, or more particularly the line of Ikshvaku.

This blood gradually spread until it has come down "to many who are by descent people of the land." Thus there is no hard-and-fast line of demarcation between nobility and common folk. There cannot be as long as nobles and common folk intermarry, and nobility is transmitted through the mother as much as, if not more than, through the father. There are signs, however, that Fiji was tending in the same direction as India when we arrived in the country; the nobility of great states tended to isolate themselves and to marry amongst themselves. British

[1] *Lau*, 219.

G

rule, with its intense snobbery, is accentuating this tendency, because it courts the highest and ignores the rest.

The non-noble clans are often referred to as "the Land."[1] As usual, however, this word is loosely used. It has a more precise meaning when it refers to the inferior side of the village; for noble villages are often divided into two parts by a stream; on the one side lives the nobility with the clans more intimately connected with it; the other is the Land. But then we find that the non-noble clans on the side of the nobility are referred to as the Land in relation to the nobles. Finally, the word is used of villages outside the capital, and could sometimes be translated the peasantry.

The Land in the first sense is a very honourable estate, attending on the king, supporting him, punishing slights, and being his mainstay in battle. They recall the *Maruts*, so that we may provisionally equate them with the Indian *vis*, or third caste.[2]

Outside the capital there are villages of an honourable standing, some related to the nobility. There are also villages that are "low-born," "very low-born," or "low at the bottom."[3]

To take a concrete example: In Lakemba there is the capital with the king and the court dignitaries. There are besides two villages that rank as noble because their chiefs are supposed to be of the same stock as the nobility. A fourth village is not of that stock, but it is not low; it has a headman with an honoured title who sits with the court officials at great assemblies, though obviously humbler than they in his demeanour. A fifth village is lower, but still fairly honourable as holding the position of "border" which is sometimes identical with that of

---

[1] *Vanua.*   [2] Above, p. 39.

[3] *Kaisi, kaisi sara, kaisi mbotomboto. Lau,* 5, 236.

"land" in the narrow sense of the word. Finally, there come two villages that are lowborn, not relatively, but absolutely. They had no proper chiefs but were subject to other villages. At feasts they swept away the rubbish, and drove off the dogs.

Thus it would be possible to evolve out of Fijian society a three-caste system:

> Nobility (*Turaña*=Indian *Kshatriya*).
> Land (*vanua*=Indian *viś*).
> Serfs (*Kuisī sara*=Indian *sudra*).

I do not say that such a system exists or that it would have evolved. My point is that the Fijian system is still in a fluid state out of which it would be possible to crystallize several social schemes, of which here is one. All that is necessary is to stop intermarriage at a certain line. Stop it between nobles and the rest, and you get a closed nobility as in India; let the people of the land refuse to marry with serfs and you get a well-defined farmer caste and a serf caste. We have observed such a tendency in the nobility, though not in the commons.

V

Since the status of the clans is determined by the office they hold about the king or chief, they are best studied through the bearers of those offices.

At the head of the system is the king or high chief. His Fijian title is *Sau*, which means "peace," "prosperity." In practice he is vaguely referred to as "The *Turaña*," the lord, or chief. He generally has a territorial title which consists of *Tū* or *Tui*, e.g. *Tū Vuma*, Lord of Vuma, *Tui Nayau*, Lord of Nayau.[1] This is not peculiar to kings

---

[1] *Tū*, to stand; *tui*, to stand in.

and high chiefs, however, for village headmen and clan chieftains bear such titles.

The king receives the state offerings. That, not ruling, is the essence of his function. When a chiefless tribe of south-western Vanua Levu decided to have a chief it was "in order that he might face the feasts." He can be constantly seen facing the feasts—that is, he sits with his chieftains, and offerings are brought to him, offered up with a prayer, touched and acknowledged with a prayer by his herald on his behalf. He sits and receives the *kava* draught, which is to Fiji what *soma* is to India. Kava drinking is his daily occupation.

He resembles the Indian sacrificer in so far as he is the head of the ritual and the person consecrated thereby, but he differs from the Vedic king in being much more passive. The Vedic king has often to act, to carry the fire pan, to brandish a wooden sword, to run a race even; the Fijian king just sits. It must be remembered, however, that there are other rituals in India, pre-Aryan probably, in which the king is so passive that his place can be taken by an idol, in which action belongs entirely to the priest.

I will not undertake here a comparative analysis of the Indian and the Fijian royal ritual, because I have done so elsewhere.[1] I shall be content to point out that the principle is the same. Both kings stand for the gods; but whereas in India the theory is very definite, the king is Indra, Varuna, later Siva or Vishnu, and other gods, in Fiji all is vague, and the theory of divine kingship is all inference confirmed by rare direct statements, such as this one: "In the olden times it was the chief who was our god." Or this: "Only the chief was believed in; he was by way of being a human god. Spirits were only useful in war; in other things, no." In all my wanderings and inquiries only once have I heard him identified with

[1] *Kingship*, VII *ff*. Since then further details could be added.

definite gods. That was in Tokatoka. There the chief represents the tribal god and all the clan gods, his sons, who are the same as their father. That is exactly what the king was in Vedic India; he was Indra, but he was other gods as well, and those gods, or their powers, were deposited in Indra.[1] We must assume that there was once a more definite theory at the back of the divine kings of Fiji; for men begin with definite ideas which they work out, until a routine is established of which the meaning fades. It has so faded in Fiji that we can scarcely see it.

Why should the Fijians want a god represented in the flesh? Why should anyone? The Fijians have given us one reason: he was, in things other than war, useful above the priests who were possessed by the gods; he was useful for prosperity, as his title indicates, for good crops and good fishing.[2] The test of a lucky king is sometimes a good haul of fish for the feast of his installation. He was not a fighting man. Even in the affairs of peace he was not very active, but had a second, a kind of commander, "to carry the kingship," as they put it, to see that the feasts were brought and that the people did their service to the king.[3]

As for the deliberative side, it was in the hands of the elders. They sat with him drinking kava and deciding the affairs of the land.[4]

If the king himself, "being old and white-haired, stayed at home," the younger members of the nobility were turbulent and responsible for most of the fighting. They had to be restrained by the chieftains who held office at court.

[1] *Sat. Br.*, III, 4, 2, 15. *Ait. Br.*, I, 24. *Kings and Councillors*, 88 *ff*.
[2] *Kingship*, IV, V.
[3] *Lau*, 52.
[4] By "deciding the affairs of the land" I translate *lewā na vanua*. *Lewā* might be more concisely translated "rule," but that would introduce European implications foreign to Fijian society.

VI

The chieftains are the titled heads of the clans directly vassal to the king, and the headmen of the villages directly subject to him.[1]

These chieftains are called *masi* or *mata ni vanua*.

Masi means bark-cloth. In consecrating a chief, a strip of cloth is tied round his arm or waist, hence the title.[2]

The phrase *mata ni vanua* is more difficult to interpret, but we have prepared the way. Literally it means "face," "eye," "front of the land." Of this term I have never heard an explanation, but fortunately the people of Vanua Levu use the term quite differently, not of a personage, but of the sacred land of the tribe, a plot, the place of the ancestor god, whence the tribe is said to have arisen, and which is never cleared.[3] The term "face of the land" is explained as "the landing place of the gods, their entrance, where they come up." It is the burial place of the ancestor. In Koroalau *mata* by itself means grave. Elsewhere in Vanua Levu a grave is called "the face of the spirits" or "the face of the shrine of the spirits."[4] It is synonymous with "face of the grave" or "face of the underworld."[5] I suggest that the chieftains of the Koro Sea Tribes are identified with the grave or tumulus, the abode of the gods, naturally, if the god or gods abide in

[1] As soon as we try to generalize in Fiji we have to be vague since there are all kinds of local differences, as there are all degrees of centralization. The greater the centralization, the more the subject villages sink, while the heads of clans round the king rise. The above statement represents fairly the state of affairs in Lakemba, and probably Lau in general, but does not necessarily apply to Viti Levu.

[2] *Lau*, 67, 223.

[3] In Ceylon the sacred city of Anuradhapura was "the face of the land" (*bhūvadana*), *Mhvs.*, XI, 4. Professor M. A. Canney tells me the "face" figures in the Old Testament to a degree that is unfortunately disguised by our translations.

[4] *Mata ni tevoro, mata ni sava ni tevoro.*

[5] *Mata ni mbulu. Mbulu,* to bury, grave, underworld.

them. To those not familiar with Fiji this may seem far-fetched, but fortunately we have definite evidence from a petty tribe near Mbau, within the borders of the Koro Sea culture. Their god was called "Lord in the Grave";[1] their chief was entitled "Face of the Grave"[2] "on account of the Lord in the Grave."[3] This brings Fijian thought close to Indian thought. The Fire-god Agni is identified with the priesthood, but also with the altar and the tumulus. Thus the Fijian equation

$$\text{chieftain} = \text{tumulus,}$$

because both are the abode of the god, can be paralleled with the Indian equation

$$\text{priest} = \text{tumulus.}[4]$$

Finally in Wailevu we have a herald whose title is "From the departing place of the souls of the dead."[5]

In Lau these chieftains are more commonly called *matapule*, a Polynesian word which can be translated approximately "face of worship," "of prayer," but only approximately. The Indian word *brahman* would probably come nearer to *pule*.[6]

[1] *Ratumaimbulu.*

[2] *Matanimbulu.*

[3] Fison translated *mata ni vanua* "eye of the land," and drew a parallel with Darius' inspectors, his "eyes and ears." But these "faces of the land" have nothing to do with inspecting. So far from travelling about to report, they always sit with the chief and talk and deliberate. The Fijians never connect them with the king's eyes, but with his speech. This is one of those inspirations which appeal by their ingenuity, and so are circulated round clubs and drawing-rooms till they become received opinion, but which are never put to the test. Works on Fiji are only too full of them.

[4] *Kings and Councillors,* 19, 186, 228, 64.

[5] *Ko mai Nai* ✕ *imba* ✕ *imba. Lau,* 184.

[6] *Matapule* is etymologically the same as the Fijian *matámbure*, but the meaning of *pule* is not that of *mbure*. I should not like to decide at present which is the earlier meaning, "temple" or "prayer." It is just possible the original meaning of *matapule* is "face of the temple," hence chieftain, hence a clan.

Their title is the only evidence we have that these chieftains are the representatives of the god. Nowhere else do I find any hint of this. They are not the priests in whom the clan gods enter and who prophesy concerning disease and war. They belong to another cycle, an older one, the state ritual in which possession plays no part and of which the king is the head. It is a system of which the mechanism has become very vague but of which the purpose is quite clear, prosperity.[1]

The chieftains and their clans originally owned the land. We have statements, made independently in different places, that the nobility used to own no land, but had come into the possession of land by way of dowries which women of the land (that is women of non-noble clans) brought with them when they married noblemen. Another way in which the nobility got land was by the noble children of such women begging some from their maternal relations.[2] In one tribe of Vanua Levu the chief was said to have no land, but to get his food from one particular clan. In one tribe it appeared at first sight that the nobles owned all the land, but on analysis it was found that the term *turaṅa* was being used, as so often, in the sense of notables. As a matter of fact, the chieftains owned most of the land, "because they were the owners of the land, but land was conveyed to other clans by marriage."[3]

These statements help us to understand certain statements of the old Indian ritualists; for it was as true of

---

[1] Only in Varata do I find anything more definite. There the herald was also "priest of rain and sun." Making rain and sunshine probably lies at the base of all prosperity cults, but in Fiji rain-making has almost completely disappeared. *Kings and Councillors*, 54 *ff*., V.

[2] *Lau*, 97 *f*.

[3] Lit. "by the sister's son" (*vasu*). See *Progress of Man*, 259 *f*. This landlessness of the nobles may be connected with the belief of the people of Suva that the crops would wither if their king went into the fields.

ancient Fiji as of ancient India that "the king is an eater, the chieftains are food."[1]

The nobles may rank higher than the chieftains, and figure largely in the wars, but in the state ritual the younger ones have no place. A noble youth would not be present with the chieftains at the king's *kava*, except to make the *kava* and to wait on them. A nobleman could not fight in their presence, and they were intercessors with the king.[2]

VII

Among these "faces of the land" there is one that stands out as "The Face of the Land." When Fijians speak of "the face of the land" in the singular, they generally mean one particular chieftain whom I shall call the herald.[3] In the great states of Rewa, Verata and others he is called "The Great Face of the Land."

The heralds of Mbau were very great people. In a story of old times one of them says to an ambassador, "I dispose of all the children of the war chiefs, whether they should

[1] Above, p. 40.

[2] *Lau*, 54 *f.*

[3] In my *Lau Islands* I took this to be the original meaning, since it was usual; its application to other chieftains I imagined was an extension, a loose usage. The evidence of Vanua Levu and Viti Levu have since driven me to the view adopted above. This shows the importance of recording the exact words of the people, as otherwise any misinterpretations cannot be corrected subsequently. Had I been content to report only my conclusions, I could never have discovered the errors; as it is, I have noted the native statements word for word and translated them consistently. Thus the word "herald" always stands for *mata ni vanua*. It is always open to the critical reader to translate it back as *mata ni vanua*, and then re-translate it "chieftain" if he thinks my translation does not fit the context. This will rarely be necessary in Lau, since *mata ni vanua* is scarcely ever used there of any but the herald; the chieftains are generally referred to as *matāpule*. Re-translation will, however, frequently be needed in my manuscript for the rest of Fiji.

marry or not."[1] In free states he comes next to the king in rank, but that is not invariably the case; in Lakemba, for instance, two other chieftains claim to be more potent as peacemakers;[2] but whether higher or lower, he is always nearest to the king. He sits beside him and is constantly with him. So close is the association that he is allowed to eat the king's leavings, a thing allowed to no one else except the king's wife. He always drinks *kava* immediately after the king, but his cup is not reckoned as a distinct one. What the Fijians call the second cup is the one after the herald.

His functions in Somosomo are described as follows: "To speak to the king and receive the answer, and to proclaim the king's decision. Concerning going or staying, or feasts, or gifts, it is his duty to proclaim the decision and to report the reports of all the men who want to see the king."[3] Seated beside the king, he touches on his behalf the food and gifts offered to him, and prays over them for comfort and welfare. "He does not divide the feast; he is the king's second; he gives out the king's word; he decides where the feast can be divided; he points out to the small 'faces of the land' the shares." He is not merely a channel of communication, but, rather, submits his own decisions to the king. In one small tribe "he speaks in state affairs; the chiefs just hear his report. He just tells them what he has done; he assesses the feast, and the chiefs hear the assessment he has decided: if it is too small the chief increases it." If his chief is making offerings to a suzerain or to a friendly chief, it is he who carries out the presentation, apologizes for the smallness, and entreats the recipient's indulgence.

[1] The war chief of Mbau was not the highest in rank, but the most powerful chief in the whole of Fiji, and became recognized by the Europeans as king of Fiji.

[2] *Lau*, 54.

[3] *Na Mata*, 1911, 182*b*.

Speaking is the most characteristic function, and so he is spoken of as "the speech of the chiefs." One described himself to me as "the mouth of my king."

The Fijian herald has thus much in common with the Indian chaplain: he controls the ritual; he is the active partner; he is almost like a wife, and speech is his part. He is master of ceremonies and minister. He is not, however, as fully differentiated from the other chieftains as the brahman is from the chiefs of clans (*vis*). In the absence or incapacity of the herald, other chieftains may act in his stead. An extinct family of heralds can be replaced by another clan, whereas the nobility, if extinct, cannot be replaced, except by importing noble blood. He is a peacemaker; no nobleman may fight in his presence; but in Lakemba he shares that prerogative with two other chieftains. In the bigger states there is a specialization of functions. Some have an outdoor herald who "speaks out of doors" and an indoor herald "who does not speak outside"; in other words, one directs all ceremonial on the village green or in front of Big House; the other deals with offerings brought into Big House.[1] This distinction of indoor and outdoor, inside and outside, will appear again; but it must be noted that to officiate out of doors is not inferior as it is at the Temple of the Tooth. On the contrary, the outdoor herald is the great herald. The great herald of Rewa has a second called Questioner,[2] because if the discussion between the herald and the king lasts long, he inquires, "What has been decided by you gentlemen?"

VIII

Among the Koro Sea tribes the herald is never wanting. The other offices vary, sometimes in title rather than in function.

[1] *Lau*, 53 f.   [2] *Tarotaro*.

In every tribe there is one chieftain who with his people dresses the chief's head, watches over his corpse, and buries him. Sometimes it is the herald, sometimes a separate clan known variously as *mbota, mbouta, mbauta,* or "holy hand" or "hand of the holy thing."[1] To understand the need of such an official, we must remember that the king's body, especially his head, is sacred; to touch it is to court disease. A special officer therefore is needed. Even he may not touch his food with his hands until purified. If there is no special office the herald seems to be indicated, since he stands in such a close relationship to the king.

This function we may by way of hypothesis identify with that of barber. Here it may be objected: "You have already supposed

"Fijian herald=Indian barber;

now you propose

"Fijian holy hand=Indian barber.

You cannot have it both ways." We have just seen, however, that in Fiji the herald and the official who dresses the king's head are not always the same; there has been differentiation, just as Indian evidence has suggested a differentiation between brahmans and potters.[2] The personages are at bottom all priests who have specialized in different ways; and that is precisely where comparative evidence is so indispensable, because it enables us to trace that differentiation in a way which would be impossible if we confined ourselves to India or any one country. Fijian society is especially valuable,

[1] *Liña tambu, liña i ni ka tambu.* Yet another term is *vunikualo. Vu* means god, but the priest is identified with the god. So we may translate "priest of the spirit," "mortuary priest."

[2] Above, p. 14.

because the differentiation has not gone far yet. The
tribe of Rewa provides us with an interesting stage.
There the "Great Face of the Land," the herald, only
attends the king's body until the men of the burying caste
take it away; then he leaves it. Rewa has moved somewhat in the direction of India: the herald, like the
brahman, cannot accompany the corpse, but he may
watch over it till the funeral, a thing the brahman cannot
do.[1]

A further differentiation is to be observed in the state
of Ndreketi, in Vanua Levu. There besides the herald
there are two kinds of *mbota*, the "noble *mbota*," who
come next to the nobles in rank, and the "*mbota* to the
grave," who are of lower rank. The first touched the
living chief's head; to be allowed to touch their food,
they had only to take a stone and throw it away. Their
inferior colleagues, after touching his head, had to make a
feast called "the washing of the hands" before they could
touch their food. In another tribe, those who touch the
king from the waist downwards are differentiated.

The absence of washermen in Fiji is easily accounted
for: bark cloth, the only cloth, does not wash.

IX

There is always a chief of the border, though his clan
does not always appear under that name.

The term wants explaining. The Fijian name is *mbati
ni vanua* (short *mbati*), tooth, edge, rim, border. Function
sheds no light on the origin of this term. The only explanation I have been offered is that "they stand on the
edge; the nobles [or chiefs] lean upon them."[2] The remark
is obscure, but it at all events assures us that the Fijian
has in mind a border, and not a tooth.

[1] Above, p. 11.   [2] *Lau*, 56.

We are thus reduced to conjecture. It is natural to see in the word a contrast to *mata*, eye, face, centre. The border then would be the people who are on the periphery of the land, as opposed to the centre, the land in the sense of the sacred land, not of the whole country. It is the common Fijian contrast of inside and outside. It agrees with this that in two tribes the border people stand outside Big House while the king is being consecrated inside, with, of course, his "great face of the land" by his side. Big House, be it remembered, is built on a plinth of earth which is indistinguishable from the mound or tumulus on a grave.[1] The face of the land and the border would then be the shrine and the precincts.

The border people are the mainstay of the king. They are his last hope when he is hard-pressed. They not only smite external enemies for him, but also those subjects who are insolent or disobedient. They always take the lead: they go ahead in war and in games, they get the head of the pig, sometimes their share of a feast is called out first and their chief drinks the second cup of *kava* (i.e. next to the herald, whose cup is not counted).[2] In some places the vanguard is called "divine face of the army," in others "face of the god."[3] That enables us to understand and believe the old Indian ritualist when he tells us that the fire god is the face of the gods, the army leader the face of the army.[4] In Fiji any division of an army is a "face of the army," and the vanguard is the god-face. There is nothing esoteric about it; it is common knowledge.

I think here we have a decisive detail, one which

---

[1] Hocart, "On the Meaning of the Word Kalou," *J.R.A.I.*, 1912, 437.

[2] Above, p. 90. *Lau*, 25, 56, 78, 222. *Na Mata*, 1912, 174, 182.

[3] *Mataivalu kalou, mata ni kalou*. *Kalou* means god, spirit, spirit of the dead.

[4] *Sat. Br.*, V, 3, 2, 1.

enables us to equate with confidence the Indian army leader with the Fijian chieftain of the vanguard.

The title "Sir Border"[1] does occur, but, curiously enough, in those very parts where the institution is obscure or not well developed. Round the Koro Sea he bears such titles as Spar, Spar-of, Arm-ring[2] (because a man puts on a shell ring when he has slain his first victim). In one case he is called "grandfather of the club," for as king's champions his clan is closely connected with the club.[3] He is then a warlike personage, in contrast to the king and the herald.

X

In every village there is an open space surrounded by temples and houses of the great. This village green is called *rārā*, that is "the place below," as viewed from the plinth on which the houses are built and from which the king and his chieftains survey feasts, presentations, and dances. One gets the impression that there is a sanctity about it, though it is difficult to point to any concrete evidence. It is the *agora* or *forum* of the Fijians.

Most tribes have an official who officiates on this green. He bears the title Lord of the Green. He arranges the portions of the feast as decided by the herald, and he calls out the names of the recipients. Hence he is in some places called "Sir Crier."[4]

There is often a clan known as *mbete*. The word can be translated priest, with the proviso that his priesthood consists in being possessed by the god and in prophesying, usually concerning war and sickness. The term is thus

[1] *Roko Mbati.*

[2] *Takala, Takalai, Tora.* The *takala* is some spar or boom which I cannot at present identify; but it was explained that it supported the hull as he the chief.

[3] *Lau,* 144, 223.

[4] Ro Kaðikaið.

much narrower than our term "priest." The anthropologists would call him a shaman, which is perhaps a better term and avoids confusion; for we have come to the conclusion that all the chieftains are in a sense priests. They are not possessed, like the shaman, but merely officiate in a prosperity cult of which the king is the head. Besides this cult of the king, there is the cult of the clan gods, for each of whom there is a shaman. The head of the clan need not be the shaman; I doubt if he ever is; anyhow he must be a man capable of being possessed, going hysterical, we should call it. This cult belongs, as I have said, to quite a different cycle from the state ritual, and there is evidence that it is a late comer from the west.

Though every clan has its shaman, there is one who is The Shaman, just as all chieftains are faces of the land, but there is one who is The Face of the Land. I have not yet been able to distinguish by analysis what marks The Shaman off from other shamans, but they seem to be connected with war, and to be the shamans of the god most potent in war, for that is the function of the gods.

The "house folk"[1] deserve some mention, because it is possible to identify them with an Indian status.

They cook for the king (at least in Lakemba) after the manner of women; for men cook out of doors in hot stones, but it is the part of the women and "the house folk" to cook indoors with pots. The Lord of Nayau's house folk even carry loads on their backs like women, whereas men carry them on a stick. Yet their position is an honourable one and their privileges a matter of boast. In other cases they are said to be "exceedingly low-born," "the chief's very own men"—in other words, serfs. What marks them all, high or low, is that they are directly under the king, and not under a chieftain who is vassal to the king. This shows itself in the privilege they enjoy

[1] *Kai vale.*

of walking straight into Big House and making themselves at home, cooking food and giving to any stranger who comes to Big House. On the other hand, they were entirely at the king's mercy. I met such a man whom his lord used to beat whenever he was out of humour with one of his chieftains, "For," he would explain, "you are my man. I can kill you if I like." We can say of these serfs what the Indian text says of the fourth caste: that "they are killable at will."

It must not be imagined that these house folk are permanently attached to Big House, that they are the servants at Big House. It is not an occupation: it is a status. Take the Lord of Nayau, for instance: the whole of the island of Nayau, several hundred souls, were his house folk; they lived in their island and went about the usual avocations of Fijians. The king's household consisted of young ladies, one at least the king's own cousin, and there was only one woman, if I remember right, who came from Nayau. All the title of "house folk" meant was that if the Nayau people came to Lakemba they had certain duties and privileges. Presumably, if the king were short in his household, Nayau would be the place to send to for a kitchen wench.

Like the so-called jaggery men of Ceylon, then, these house folk are men who owe service, not professional and habitual cooks.

XI

In fact, all these offices are purely ceremonial. They all form part of the king's state, and the king's state is an organization for prosperity by the due observance of traditional rules.

There are, however, clans which specialize as craftsmen, and which at first sight might be thought to owe

H

their status to a special knowledge of that craft. A close examination will, however, dispel appearances.

The first thing to note is that these craftsmen are no part of the original scheme. The carpenters, fishermen and navigators are invariably foreigners whose place of origin is known. Some come from Tonga, some from the north coast of Viti Levu; one carpenter family came from Samoa.[1]

The second point is that these technicians are quite superfluous as far as industry goes. They might die out and canoes and houses would continue to be built, fish to be caught, and canoes to be navigated as before. As a matter of fact, the carpenters are extinct in Somosomo, and the navigators of Lakemba have given up navigating and taken to agriculture. The only thing that suffers is the king's state.

"Anyone," I was told, "can build a paddling canoe and there is no ceremony; but large sailing canoes are put into the hands of carpenters, and there are feasts at the various stages of the construction." The clue to this distinction is that the large double canoes are "sacred canoes" in which the king goes on his progresses.

If a man wishes to build a house, his kinsmen help him. The finer work is left to a carpenter—not necessarily a carpenter by birth. One of the best carpenters I knew, one who held strong views on truth in art, was just an ordinary agriculturist. Any man who has the skill may undertake the work; sometimes those who have none offer their services with an eye to the pork and gifts that are the reward of carpentry; hence the saying, "A carpenter who wants to eat pork," of a man who professes for the sake of gain to be able to do what he cannot. The hereditary carpenters are the king's carpenters; they build Big House and temples. The nobles and land folk can beg for

[1] *Lau*, 18, 55, 204. Above, p. 80.

their services, if they can afford the necessary feasts.[1]
It is easy to see how by gradual extension a king's
carpenter may become the community's carpenter, but
Fiji has not yet reached that state. If the king's state
declines, as it has done under our rule, the carpenters
and other technicians are not taken over by the community, but become absorbed in the mass of agriculturists.

Every Fijian can sail. I have sailed from one island to
another with a crew of schoolboys, and felt safer than with
a crew of grown-up amateurs in our country. No one needs
navigators except the king. To sail his sacred canoe, he
has a family or village which holds the office of navigator.

Boys begin to spear fish or use a line from an early age:
it is their play. The women begin as girls to share in the
most important form of fishing, which is with nets. Everyone is a fisherman. The fisher clans are the king's fishermen. In the words of a Fijian "the fisher boys are vassals
to the suzerain land. The various suzerain lands have
fisher boys. It is the duty of the fisher boys to carry out
the *corvée*, to go out for turtle or fish, as the order may
come from their suzerain land."[2] Note that the Fijians,
like the Sinhalese and Tamils, associate caste with vassalage and that they fish only by order of the chief. The
order is conveyed by a hereditary envoy-to-the-fishermen,
just as any request or order to a foreign or vassal state. It
is conveyed with gifts which are offered to the chief
fisherman with the usual prayer. The leaders of the fishing
party are called "the spirits" or "gods of the turtle,"[3]
evidently because they are the vehicles of the spirits of
fishing. The day before the fishing the chieftain carries
out divination with coconuts, each of which belongs to a

[1] *Lau*, 55, 131.
[2] *Na Mata*, 1914, 21 f.
[3] *Kalou ni vonu*. I must remind the reader that the Fijians make no
distinction between spirits of the dead and gods, unless they particularly
want to.

particular god. After the divination there is a thank-offering. The chieftain's provisions are put into a "sacred basket." At sea they use divination once more to know the pleasure of the gods. There are many observances which justify us in adapting to Fijian fishermen our Tamil friend's description of a barber, and in saying that "they are priests on the fishing ground." In fact, the chief fisherman's title is sometimes *matāpule*, "face of prayer, of worship." Technically he is superfluous; ritually he cannot be dispensed with.

In Suva there is specialization in fishing. The king's carpenters go turtling, the "water folk"[1] catch fish. The way it came about is that the carpenters taught the water folk to build canoes, and in return the fishermen taught the carpenters how to fish. Fiji is far from having realized the advantages of specialization. Here is a case of de-specialization, of rationalization, one might call it, where two castes find it to their advantage to combine connected crafts, fishing and the making of canoes in which to fish.

Bark-cloth is made by the women at large, so is oil. Women's crafts obviously cannot be a basis of caste, since women do not hold office.

The only craft that is not plied by all the people is pottery. It is confined to a few villages in Fiji, and dies with them, not like the chieftainship because of heredity, but for the simple reason that the technique is not handed on.[2] It is significant that this, the only craft which is entirely in the hands of specialists, has not become the basis of a caste. Ask a Fijian what is the status of a clan, he will tell you it is noble, border, herald, carpenter, or as the case may be, but never potter. One reason is that pot-making is a pure craft, not a ritual, and pots have no ceremonial associations. Feasts are cooked in hot stones,

[1] *Kai wai.*   [2] *Lau,* 18.

and so it is the oven of hot stones that has a place in social organization and its language, not the pot.[1] An additional reason among the Koro Sea Tribes is that there the industry is in the hands of the women, generally of the navigating or fishing castes.

XII

The technical castes thus turn out to be ritual, like the others. They differ only in being accretions to the ritual organization. They seem to belong to a different culture. We have noted that the king's carpenters alone have that peculiarity of Indian caste of not intermarrying or interdining.

They come nearer to India also in respect of land. The purely Fijian castes all owned land, except the nobles long ago. The technical castes owned no land. As one tribe put it, "the fishermen's planting is in the sea." The whole of the reef in this case was divided into parts of which the sea folk each owned his bit. Some fishermen got vegetable food by barter, others were fed by the chiefs. In Mbau the king's carpenters planted in the land of their masters, which is rather like Ceylon. On the other hand the Tongan carpenters and the fishermen of Lakemba were given land to dwell on only. They did not cultivate, but were given the right to seize food from any fields in return for the work they did. Besides, they received offerings at every stage of their work.[2] These offerings correspond to the fees of the Sinhalese barber or washerman.[3]

---

[1] Oven is a term for a social division, a clan. Above, p. 78.
[2] *Lau* 55, 125 *f.*, 129.   [3] Above, p. 44.

XIII

We saw that if we exclude these technical castes as no part of the scheme, we can make out roughly three estates, nobility, faces of the land and village headmen, serfs. Or, rather, these are possible lines of cleavage. Further, we saw that among the faces of the land there is one who stands somewhat apart. That is another line of cleavage. I would not venture to say positively in which direction Fijian society was tending when we arrived on the scene. On the whole it would seem to have tended rather towards the exaltation of the nobility and the consequent lowering of the other estates. There is good evidence of this in Lau.[1] However that is an academic question, since Fiji has not been allowed to develop its own way. Our coming has definitely exalted the higher ranks of the nobility over all the other classes, which in consequence have all been reduced to one level. Below the nobility a new class has been created, a black-coated middle class of Government servants, which must tend to squeeze out the nobility as it has so often done.

XIV

To return to the system as it used to be. The Fijians have no theories as to its origin, but many tribes have some idea how particular families came to hold particular offices. The hill tribes of Viti Levu tell about an installation ceremony at which the ancestor was installed as chief and laid down certain customs. This installation is said by some tribes to be the occasion on which the tribe was divided up into settlements, and a chieftain was appointed to each division.

Until I have worked out my notes on this region I cannot give more details about these traditions, but I can

[1] *Lau*, 204, 236.

give one example from the Rewa Delta. The tribe of Rewa now hold the title of Noble Lord of Ndreketi, one of the three or four highest in Fiji, but it was not always theirs; it belonged to the original inhabitants. For the Rewans came down the river like so many other tribes. The king of the original inhabitants bestowed his title on the leader of the newcomers. He did so at an installation ceremony at which he also fixed the status of his own people as serfs to the newcomers; to another village he gave the right to instal the king, and assigned to each clan the privileges it holds to the present day.

The Fijians too believe that the king fixes privileges; but we know too much about the growth of societies to believe in the sudden creation of a social organization. These legends cannot commemorate what never can happen, but only the readjustment and confirmation of an existing system.

The king can, for instance, adopt strangers into the State and fix their duties. Such has been the case with all the technical castes. He awards privileges which increase the prestige of clans. Thus the Lord of Lakemba is fabled to have adopted fugitives from Mbau as his navigators and to have given them the right, which they still hold, of wearing the turban in his presence. More recently a high chief gave a Tongan navigator the right to the second cup of *kava*.[1]

To the present day vacancies among the court offices are filled by the king at his installation. He is bound by the rules of heredity, but not rigidly. In Lakemba the king's herald also enjoyed the title of Envoy to Mbau; but the line had fallen into disfavour, and this seems to have coincided with a tendency for the nobility to reserve themselves high titles. So Finau at his installation appointed one of his kinsmen his Envoy to Mbau, and in

[1] *Lau*, 63, 54. Above, p. 90.

public functions constantly preferred another chieftain for the duties of herald. Public opinion, however, did not recognize this departure from the true line, and continued to address the herald as "envoy to Mbau," and to speak of his clan as "the heralds."[1]

One tradition recalls a common type of Indian legend. The house of the Lord of Yaro was originally noble, but once they cooked a turtle (a privilege reserved to the chief); therefore the chief smote them, so that they have declined to the present day.[2]

Thus in Fiji, as in India and in Persia, the king appears as the head of the caste system, confirming officers in their offices, promoting or degrading.

XV

In filling vacancies caused by the extinction or inefficiency of the rightful holders, the king cannot act arbitrarily. When Finau set aside the rightful herald, as I have related, he did not substitute the first-comer, but turned to the female line. His nominee was, however, poor at speaking, so on all occasions when eloquence and self-confidence were required another chieftain was preferred. The king had to fall back on the nearest, seniority being a guiding principle.

It is a settled conviction of the Fijians that the first-born is chief. There are, however, exceptions. I spent most of my time in a state in which the junior line had seized the power, but this was noted as abnormal.

In many tribes there are two chiefs. If you ask the reason why, they suppose that they represent the descendants of two brothers.

In Western Viti Levu it was laid down that "the custom of the Fijians is that the first-born is strong. The old men

[1] *Lau*, 53, 54, 67.   [2] *Lau*, 228.

say the first-born has the club, the bow, the younger brother speaks the word."[1] It is the relationship of Santanu and Devapi, only in the Indian story the seniority was reversed by an unnatural usurpation, as it is sometimes in Fiji.[2] I have collected elsewhere evidence that the relations of king and herald are very similar to those of elder and younger brother.[3]

The tribes of Western Viti Levu have no exact equivalent of the eastern herald. If you inquire after the herald, they produce the chief's messenger, an office not nearly so honourable. They say, "The youngest branch are servants, make food for the chiefs and are sent on errands." In one place they call this messenger "the sheet-of-cloth," a term applied to the last born, because a piece of cloth is first cut off for the eldest then for the next, the youngest getting what is left. These messengers seem to us to be more like the house folk of the eastern tribes. Anyhow, they are proof that servitude may be based, not on conquest, but on seniority.

In Rewa the king looks upon his border clan as his younger brothers. His queen also has her border clan: it is the fourth and youngest branch of the nobility, descendants of the younger brothers of the ancestors of the king's house. They hold this office because the youngest of several brothers is sent on errands, and so therefore are his descendants.

You can observe this servitude by seniority any day in any Fijian family of rank. The authority of the eldest brother is paramount; the younger ones do his bidding, wait for their food till he has finished his, do not speak unless spoken to. At a *kava* party if there is no member of

---

[1] Below, p. 122.

[2] Above, p. 45.

[3] "Fijian Heralds and Envoys," *J.R.A.I.*, 1913, 110 *ff*. I there assumed the heraldship to have originated in Fiji, but comparative evidence makes this untenable.

a chieftain's house present a junior noble acts as master of ceremonies. A cadet of a noble house will describe himself as low-born in relation to his senior.

Quite definitely, then, the Fijians consider the status of a house to depend on seniority, and we need no longer strain at the Indian view that the low caste is junior, later born.[1] The exclusive study of Indian texts led us, as usual, into hopeless scepticism. Comparative study has brought us back to a simple confidence. Not that the Indian pedigrees are necessarily correct: they may be forged; but if you forge a pedigree you must make it plausible, and to make an Indian pedigree plausible you must evidently derive the castes from brothers according to some rule of seniority.

Naturally, there are conquests, and naturally the conquered are enrolled among the serfs; but there were serfs before the conquest.

XVI

It is not only the brother relationship that determines the status. Thus the social structure of Rewa comprises a "uterine nephew line."[2] Evidently they are descended from a uterine nephew of some king. Their duty is to abide with the chiefs, and convey state messages to any place the king tells them.

Rewa has also a clan called "firewood for the oven," because the king tells them to cook in an oven of hot stones. The king speaks of them as "the clan of my paternal uncles." One tribe of Vanua Levu calls the clan that buries the chief "grand-uncles of the chief."

Thus Fiji makes us understand the South Indian

[1] Above, p. 52.

[2] *Vusa Vasu*. In *Kings and Councillors* I by mistake attached to them the duties of the *vesi* bastards, who are described below, p. 107.

custom of addressing castes by terms of relationship, because the Fijians still mean it literally.[1]

XVII

Fiji also throws some little light on mixed castes. We cannot hope for much, because different ranks inter-marry freely, even the highest and lowest. Noblemen take wives from all classes in order to extend their influence, and the sons are qualified for kingship, so long as their parents have been united by arrangement of the families or states.

There are, however, bastards, sons of noblemen by kitchen wenches, or resulting from irregular unions.[2] They are called "outrigger booms,"[3] because they are attached to the true-born noblemen as a boom to the hull. Another term may be translated "sort of brother."[4] They differ in rank. The highest are termed "booms of *vesi*," because the *vesi* tree is specially affected for the canoes and houses of noblemen, being reddish in colour.[5] Their descendants are "true outrigger booms." Some-times they form separate clans, which sometimes bear the name of "the bastards."

The state of Rewa has two villages of *vesi* bastards who are exempt from ordinary corvées, such as can be foreseen, but in sudden emergencies, such as the un-expected coming of noble visitors from another tribe, they are appointed to make the feast; they will succeed "because they are noble vassals." In a neighbouring tribe the nobility is divided into four houses to each of which is attached a house of heralds who are bastards of the respective houses they serve.[5]

[1] Above, p. 53.   [2] *Lau*, 45 *f.*, 51, 52.   [3] *Ikaso*.
[4] *Ita* ✕ *ini*.   [5] Above, p. 98.
[5] This is an instance of the very common division of the royal house into four, so common that it cannot be an accident. Cp. above, p. 77.

Occasionally we come across clans which add the epithet "noble" to the description of their status. Matuku has a clan which is described as "noble" and "border." We have come across "noble *mbota*" and "mortuary *mbota*." Another tribe has noble faces of the land and common faces of the land. Presumably they are of mixed descent. It is difficult to see why they should advertise the fact in a country where almost everyone is of mixed descent, unless it is that they are descendants of a particularly great lady—an eldest daughter noble on both sides, for instance. That would make them noble indeed, without qualifying them for kingship, since succession is in the male line.[1]

XVIII

The rank of each clan depends, as we have seen, on the office filled by its head. He bears a title which very often indicates his office: Face of the Land, Lord of the Green, Sir Crier, Carpenter, and so on. The status of the clan is therefore indicated by the title of the chieftain. "What is the status of Little House?" you inquire. The answer is, "Herald." It is more usual to refer to the clan by the title of the head of the house than by its proper name. You will hear Little House more often referred to as "the heralds," or "the Envoys to Mbau." The clan of Tumbou is more generally spoken of as "the Lords of Tumbou." Thus the expression "faces of the land" is ambiguous; it may mean either the chieftains or the members of the herald clan. Thus the title belongs to the whole family, and I have heard the man who came next to the chieftain addressed by the title in the absence of the real holder.[2] The result is that the title Border has now become a description of the group, while the chieftain bears another title.[3]

[1] Cp. *Lau*, 222.   [2] *Lau*, 54.   [3] Above, p. 94.

These titles tend to become proper names. The title Lord of Tumbou was also used in the family as a proper name. This does not appear to be common, but there were to some extent family names. Thus the royal house of Lakemba was called "Fruit of the *rewa* tree." Its members affected proper names derived from that plant, such as "Rewa-shoot," "Rewa-flower." Names were often names of ancestors, especially posthumous names. After his death a nobleman was often known by a name which referred to the manner of his death, such as "Fallen in Nayau." This name would frequently pass to the next generation but one in the male line. Thus with local knowledge you might be able to guess a man's status from his name. But these cannot be regarded as caste names, since they are peculiar to the family, and not common to the caste all over an area.

Thus in the matter of names Fiji has entered on the road travelled by Ceylon, but has not gone beyond the first stage.

XIX

In some cases it seems more polite to refer to a clan as "the sons of such-and-such a chieftain." You hear of "the king's sons"[1]—not necessarily his own sons, but his brothers' sons, and the nobler members generally. The clan of Tumbou might be referred to as "the sons of the Lord of Tumbou."

More often they were referred to as "boys" or "youths."[2] I have heard men of forty referred to as "chiefly boys,"[3] but this was only used for the nobler nobles, and it had become so expressive of high rank that I have heard the king himself described as "a chiefly boy." Here Fiji differs from Ceylon where the term does

---

[1] *Luve ni San.*   [2] *None.*   [3] *None turaña.*

not apply to a consecrated king. In this case Fiji appears
to be less archaic.

The honorific nature of the term appears in the fact
that bastards of the nobility were called "bastard boys."[1]
In contrast to this, the chieftains and old men generally
were spoken of as "true chiefs."[2] Thus the term we should
expect to be higher really expresses honourable old age,
whereas the term "youth" is expressive of blue blood.

The fishermen were almost always called "fisher-
boys."[3] The term "border boys" was not quite so invariable, but was distinctly complimentary. Yet for some
obscure reason the highly honoured heralds were never
called "herald boys." It may be because they have no
proper title, but only the one of chieftain. Now a chieftain is an old man, a "true chief," so that to speak of
"chieftain boys" would be a contradiction in terms.

XX

There is no ceremony of initiation into caste. It
depends entirely on birth. There is a ceremony of installing the chieftain in his office.

It must be remembered that only the chieftain holds
office and sits in the *kava* ring.[4] In India any man of the
brahman caste can act as brahman, because every one of
them is initiated. It is quite consistent, then, that in
Fiji only the chief man should be consecrated; in India,
every member of the caste.

---

[1] *Ñone ikaso.*   [2] *Turaña ndina. Lau,* 49.   [3] *Ñone ndau.*

[4] Like all Fijian rules, this is elastic. In the absence of the Lord of
Tumbou, I have seen the senior man, who should have been Lord of
Tumbou, take his place. But no junior would do so.

XXI

Every village reproduces the state on a reduced scale.
The head of every village that is not utterly low has his
herald and his border, often nothing more; never a chief
fisherman or carpenter.[1] Thus the two offices that are
considered the minimum are purely ritual. The village
can get on without craftsmen, but not without master of
ceremonies or marshal.

When I say that a village copies the state it must not be
taken to mean that in every case the king's court came
first and all the vassal villages have imitated the suzerain.
Many of the vassal villages were once independent, or
owed a slenderer allegiance than they do now.[2] They have
not copied, but live in a reduced state. In such cases
they owe what pomp they preserve to their once having
been sovereign states. On the other hand the legends
certainly indicate that the royal organization has spread
from tribe to tribe by imitation. In either case the statement remains true that the Fijian caste system is a system
which centres in the king, and which has come to centre
also in the villages' heads. It has diffused itself throughout
the whole society, though not nearly to the same extent as
in India.

XXII

Since there are big states and little states, there must
inevitably be differences of rank within the same caste.
The member of a herald house is everywhere recognized as a herald, but that does not mean that all heralds
are equal. The heralds of Mbau and Rewa were very
great personages, greater than many vassal chiefs. I have
seen the King of the Reef's Envoy to Mbau received

[1] *Lau*, 19 ff.
[2] E.g. *Lau*, 204. There is much unpublished evidence from Lau.

with the greatest respect by the vassals on the main-
land and bearing himself as a gentleman from Court
would among country gentry. To ask a Mbauan herald
to act as master of ceremonies to the Lord of Vumā
would be like asking the Home Secretary to act as secretary to the Mayor of Puddleston.

Here we come to a great difference between the Indian
and the Fijian systems. In both a man is classified in the
same compartment wherever he goes, but whereas in
India he can attach himself to this king or that, in Fiji
he only officiates for the chief of his own land. A brahman
may be engaged by a king, or even by two kings; the
herald of the Lord of Nayau is the herald of the Lord of
Nayau from time immemorial, and of no one else. The
Fijian castes are sessile, as it were; the Indian ones free
swimming.

The difference, like all differences, is not an absolute
one. We have seen that carpenters and fishermen can
migrate and attach themselves to a new lord. The
Levukans acquired a new lord without giving up the old
one.[1] A foreign nobleman unaccompanied by a herald
would be supplied with one *pro tem*. Such a case would
probably have been rare of old, for big people did not
travel alone; but now there are many white gentlemen
who have come to Fiji without heralds, and must be
provided with one. The Governor uses the herald of the
war chief of Mbau, thus realizing the state of affairs
already reached by India as early as 800 B.C.

XXIII

As in South India, the various orders are ranged into
two divisions, only they are never associated with right
and left, but with sea and land, upper and lower.

[1] *Lau*, 69; 204 f.

A Fijian village is frequently divided into two halves separated by a stream. On the one side live the nobles. The heralds, of course, live under their wing. The other side is the Land, its inhabitants the Land folk. It either includes the border or is identical with it.[1] The Lord of the Green seems to belong to the land side, and so to go with the border.[2] That would fit in with our suggestion that the border are the outside people, whose work is on the Green as opposed to the sacred mound, the plinth of Big House or the temple, the "face of the land."

Such are the results of a general survey. To fix the position of every caste on one side or the other would require a minute analysis of my material such as it has not yet been possible to carry out. We can, however, put forward the following provisional scheme:

I. Inner and upper. The king and his "Great Face of the Land," and other chieftains who are closely attached to the king, such as those who tend his body.

II. Outer and lower. The "land folk," the border, together with the Lord of the Green, and others who do not officiate immediately round the chief; those who are on the periphery, not at the centre.

It is a feature of Fijian society that, take any community you like, it will divide into two, and each half will exhibit the same structure as the whole—that is, it will subdivide into two parts, each of which is to the other as the major divisions are to one another. And so you can go on dichotomizing down to the clan, which is divided into two sub-clans, senior and junior; inner and outer.[3] The inner holds the headship. The chieftain is therefore a small face of the land; he is to the clan what the great face of the land is to the whole community. The junior

[1] *Lau*, 10 *ff.*, 54, 221, 223, 232.
[2] Cp. *Lau*, 76 with 58 and 233.
[3] *Lau*, 232. Cp. Hocart, "Winnebago Dichotomy," *Man*, 1933, 169.

I

division is "the border of the oven," the oven being the clan, the unit of assessment.[1] It is to the clan what the border is to the community.[2]

This is not without its analogy in South India. It will be remembered that there society as a whole is divided into right and left, but so are some of the castes which are the constituent parts of that society.[3] Once again Fiji has supplied a possible key to India.

XXIV

In conclusion, the general principles of the Fijian caste system are much the same as in India: men are born to fulfil certain offices for their liege lords—offices which are necessary to the prosperity of the people. Different lineages take different offices and keep them as long as they continue to exist, or to fulfil the conditions of holding office. Sometimes a lineage will be able by force, or by push, to rise to a higher office than belongs to it by descent. These general principles are carried out in both regions with a parallelism the full extent of which awaits further investigation.

The chief difference is that India has advanced further away from feudalism in the direction of nationalization, if I may so express it. To illustrate what I mean, our kings had parks; they are still called royal parks on that account, but in fact they are now the property of the nation. Every town that has any ambition has followed suit and has its municipal park. In the same way, a great lord in Fiji has a carpenter, a fisherman, a barber, and so

[1] Above, p. 78.

[2] Actually, both halves are called "border of the oven" (*mba-ti ni lovo*) round the Koro Sea; but in Vanua Levu it is only the inferior part, the followers. I take this to be the more archaic usage, as thus alone can we make sense of the facts.

[3] Above, p. 109 *ff.*

on. In India and Ceylon we find communities provided with carpenters, potters, barbers, and so on; but the feudal character of their services is not yet lost. We shall have to go to Egypt to find a further stage from which all feudalism has completely evaporated.

In the meantime, we may sum up the results so far obtained by suggesting the following parallels—homologies I should prefer to call them—between India and Fiji:

India	*Fiji*
Nobility.	Nobility.
Brahman.	Herald.
Farmers.	Village headmen and other chieftains not yet determined.
Barber	*Mbota.*
Army leader.	Leader of the vanguard.
Cooks (jaggery men).	House folk.
Fishermen.	{ Fishermen. { Navigators.
Carpenters.	Carpenters.

Tonga

THE Tongan Islands lie to the south-east of Fiji, with which there used to be considerable intercourse.

Unfortunately, our democratizing habits have considerably obscured the organization of the lower orders. We have William Mariner's excellent account, dating from the beginning of last century, but Mariner made mistakes, and in his account of the four orders, which is so vital to us here, there are difficulties and inconsistencies.[1] These may arise out of the fact that he had not quite grasped the kinship system. Whatever the reason, it prevents us making all the capital we should like to make out of his fourfold classification into:

> *'Eiki*[2]
> *Matāpule*
> *Mu'a*
> *Tu'a*

It is only about the first two orders that I can offer any information of my own. They stand in sharp contrast to one another at the present day as nobility and masters of ceremonies.

The nobility consists of the king and the big feudal chiefs. As Mariner says, "All those persons are *egi* or nobles, or chiefs (for we have used these terms synonymously) who are in any way related to the family of Tooitonga, or Veachi, or the How."[3] They correspond to

[1] *An Account of the Natives of the Tonga Islands* (compiled and arranged by John Martin), 2nd Ed., London, 1818.

[2] Phonetically the same as Futunan *aliki*, Samoan *ali'i*, etc.

[3] *Tu'i Toña* was the supreme but powerless king. *Veachi* I found nothing about. *Ha'u* is the same as Fijian *sau*. He is the executive king who held all the power.

the Fijian nobility and Indian *kshatriya*. But Tonga was much more centralized than Fiji, and instead of number-less independent nobilities there was one nobility dis-persed through the group as vassals of varying degrees.

The term "noble boy" indicated high rank, and the king himself was addressed as "boy."

We have already met with the term *matapule* in the Windward Islands of Fiji, where it is interchangeable with the Fijian term "face of the land." In Tonga, as in Fiji, it is applied to chieftains invested with various functions. "Some of the matabooles," says Mariner, "are adepts at some art or profession, such as canoe-building, or superintending funeral rites: this last, though a cere-mony, the generality of the matabooles do not attend as it is also a distinct profession." We recognize the mortuary *mbota* of Fiji, and we note that the Tongans had the same rule as the people of Rewa, that the masters of ceremonies do not attend the king's funeral, but leave it to a special caste.[1]

One might miss those *matapules*, especially now that they are obscured or extinct, but one could not miss those whose duties are to be masters of ceremonies. The King of Tonga has two—one on his right and one on his left. These belong to different lines. There are lesser heralds attached to the feudal chiefs. They are so much masters of the ceremonies that the king himself may have to sit passive and patient while they wrangle interminably, but with dignity, about precedence. They decide who shall sit in the *kava* ring and who not. Mariner describes them as the companions of the chiefs, their "counsellors, and advisers," and thinks they "may not improperly be called their ministers."

Both the heralds drink before the king, a fact which we may compare with the Indian and Persian priests' duty of opening the ceremonies.[2]

[1] Above, p. 93.   [2] Above, pp. 39 and 72.

According to Mariner, "they are supposed to have been distant relations of the nobles or to have descended from persons eminent for experience and wisdom, and whose acquaintance and friendship on that account became valuable to the king, and other great chiefs." If they are distant relations of nobles, they must ultimately, like the Persian and Indian priests, be descended from kings. The Tongans then agree with the Fijians as regards the relationship of the two castes.

Persons may be of mixed descent. In that case they do not form a mixed caste, but pass themselves off as noble or councillor, as may suit their purpose. Thus noblemen are not allowed to sit in the king's *kava* ring. The reason seems to be that only heads of houses may sit there; the king is the head of the royal house, so no other member of it may represent the nobility. The nobles have to sit behind the bowl and fetch and carry for the councillors. To escape this, a nobleman who has councillor blood in him will take a seat in the ring. His right to do so may be queried, and he has to defend it with a pedigree.[1] In the Tongan *kava* ring, even more than in the Fijian, one realizes the meaning of the Indian saying that the sovereignty is one, the others are many.[2]

For *mu'a* and *tu'a* I depend entirely on Mariner. The first means front, the second back and is still used as a term of contempt, a low-born fellow.

Mariner says the *mu'a* have much to do in assisting at public ceremonies, "such as sharing out of food and cava under the direction of the matabooles: they sometimes arrange and direct instead of the matabooles." This variety corresponds to the Fijian lords of the green. These we classified with the border, or clan that goes in front. It is possible then that the Tongan "front men" are to be identified with the Fijian border and connected clans.

[1] *Lau*, 62.   [2] *Sat. Br.*, IX, 3, 1, 14.

Some have other duties. "Most of the mooas are the professors of some art," says Mariner. It appears then that some technicians are of chieftain or councillor rank, others are "front men."

These technicians are no more bound to follow their father's craft than their Indian compeers. "Among those that practice the arts there are many that do so because their fathers did before them. . . . There is no positive law to oblige them to follow the business of their fathers, nor any motive but the honourable estimation in which their arts are held, or their own interest, or the common custom." It is not so much a craft as an honourable office.

As such it is beyond the reach of the *tu'a* or serfs: "No person of so low a rank as a tooa can practice such respectable arts." The callings of masons, fishermen, large house builders, tattooers, club-carvers are open to both front men and serfs. Peculiar to the serfs are—

the *tufuña fair kava* (barbers or shavers with shells);
the *tañata fai umu* (cooks); and
the *kai fonua* (peasants).

"Tooas are the lowest order of all, or the bulk of the people. They are all by birth ky fonooa or peasants." Mariner describes how the second king shot down a low-born fellow who had taken the liberty of climbing a mast in presence of the executive king (for no low-born fellow can be higher than a nobleman). When Mariner remonstrated, the king explained that the man "was only a low, vulgar fellow (a cook) and that neither his life nor death was of any consequence to society."[1] They also are "killable at will."

There exists some kinship between the various orders. The "father of a chief" is a male servant.[2] It is curious that high rank is associated with youth, a humble station with age.

[1] I, 55.   [2] *Tongan Dictionary, s.v. tamaio 'eiki.*

Samoa

SAMOA recalls India by its marked dualism between the nobility and the masters of the ritual.[1]

The nobles[2] hold certain titles. There are four very big ones which, united in one person, make a king of Samoa, a vain title. So are most noble titles, since the heralds generally hold the power. Where the nobles have the upper hand, they are circumscribed by the unruliness of the people. There is so little discipline that sometimes the only way to settle a claim to a title is by awarding it to all the claimants. In one village of Savai'i, I found as many as six chiefs, all bearing the same title.

The nobility is connected with war. Councils of war consist of nobles only. The club is part of the festive apparel of a chief's son.[3]

A "chiefly boy" is one who holds high rank. Still higher is that of "chiefly offspring," which is reserved for the descendants of one particular king. The term "noble elder" is polite for "old man."[4] Once again youth and rank, age and honourable inferiority.

The title of the "herald" comes to support our interpretation of the Fijian term "face of the land."[5] It is *tulāfale*, "emplacement, plinth of the house." Thus Samoan heralds are identified with the ground on which a house stands, and we have seen that this is indistinguishable from a grave.

[1] In Samoa, as in Tonga, I must content myself with the "high lights" until a careful analysis of my notes gives a more detailed picture.
[2] *Ali'i.*
[3] *Manaia*. See Krämer, *Die Samoa-Inseln* (Stuttgart, 1902-3), I, 34.
[4] Cp. Krämer, *op. cit.*, I, 43.
[5] Above, p. 86.

We can therefore sum up the comparative evidence thus:

Brahman identified with Agni, who is the sacred fire, the altar, and the tumulus;

Fijian chieftain or councillor identified with the sacred land or tumulus;

Samoan herald identified with the emplacement, or plinth of the house.

All the talking at the assemblies held on the village green is done by the heralds, and so they appear in our literature as orators. So much is it their prerogative that it is noted as a special privilege that certain chiefs have the right to speak in certain assemblies. When these heralds or councillors speak they lean on a long staff, and hold a fly-whisk in the other hand.[1] We have again the contrast which we had in India and in Fiji between the club or sword and the staff, the insignia of war and those of speech.[2]

These heralds do not just jump up and speak when the spirit moves, like our Members of Parliament. The order of speaking is fixed by custom.[3] These are not speeches as we understand it, but ceremonial allocutions introduced by ritual greetings to every noble or herald house present, greetings which have to be learnt by heart. The speeches are in such a figurative style that they require a commentary. These heralds are the repositories of genealogies. They direct the *kava* ceremonial, award titles, and arrange the marriage of the chief's son or daughter. Such is their avarice that formerly they would get the chief married again and again for the sake of their share of the fine mats the bride brought with her. They are always

[1] Cp. Krämer, *op. cit.*, I, 43.
[2] Above, pp. 39 and 105.
[3] For some curious customs, see Krämer, I, 223.

mentioned first in the ritual greetings. Evidently going before is a characteristic not limited to the Indian chaplain. At *kava*, however, these Samoan heralds drink after the chief, not before, as is done in Tonga.

The authority of the heralds is expressed in the word *pule*, a word which we can only approximately render as prayer, worship. The chiefs on the other hand seek *mālō*, victory, hegemony. We have the same contrast as between *brahman* and *kshatra* in India.

The great heralds of the whole of Samoa, the king's electors, do not as a rule go out to fight, but stay at home praying for success. To the present day they are regarded as god-men,[1] just like the brahmans.

Chieftains other than heralds do not appear. At least I have not discovered them. Where are they? We have seen that there is no sharp distinction in Fiji between the heralds and other chieftains. All chieftains can act as masters of ceremonies, though this is generally done by the "great face of the land," while the others specialize in other duties. In Samoa chiefly titles have become so multiplied that there are almost as many chiefs as councillors, and so there cannot be a constellation of chieftains round a single chief; there are two groups, nobles and masters of ceremonies.

However that may be, there is a definite tradition of four orders, as in Tonga. Once upon a time there were four brothers who agreed to disperse and divide up their patrimony. Sana received the staff and the fly-whisk, Ana the club, Tua the digging stick, Tolufale nothing. These brothers were the eponymous ancestors of various parts of Samoa, but they evidently represent herald, noble, cultivator, and a fourth caste of which the status is not clear, since there are no insignia. Tua means "back," and presumably corresponds to the Tonga *tu'a*, the serfs;

---

[1] *Aitu tañata.*

but that is not certain. Curiously enough, he is the twin of Ana, the nobleman. Sana was the third brother.[1]

Evidently the Samoans share with the Indians and the Fijians the belief that the castes are descendants of brothers, and that status goes by seniority.

Samoa is a country where everyone wants to be somebody. I think an estimate of one title per twenty adults is not exaggerated. It reminds one of the ancient Licchavi state of Northern India, where "of the nobles dwelling in it there were always 7,707 reigning kings, as many viceroys, as many generals, and as many treasurers." "Each one thought, 'I am a king, I am a king.'"[2] No wonder that in Samoa the lower orders have disappeared, absorbed into the higher.[3]

There are personages intermediate between the chiefs and ordinary heralds. They are called herald chiefs or chiefly heralds, as the case may be.[4] The heralds, who were also noble, were the real rulers of Samoa. In Fasito'o Tai there were seven noble heralds who directed affairs, and seven chiefs who deliberated on war.

There are craftsmen,[5] carpenters and tattooers. Two families of tattooers are descendants of the two women from Fiji who are reputed to have introduced tattooing; the third family holds the office of tattooer to the Lord of *A'ana*, one of the four great titles. Their art is purely ritual. Mat-making, planting, fishing are all common property.

There are families known as "fathers of the chief."

If there is, or was, a four caste system in Samoa and in Tonga a difficult problem arises. Why could we find no

[1] Krämer, I, 27, 222.
[2] *Jataka*, I, 504; III, 1. *Lalita Vistara*, ed. Lefman, I, p. 21.
[3] I do not think I have missed them. Pratt's dictionary does not connect *mua* and *tua* with any social order.
[4] *Ali'i tulafale* and *tulafale ali'i*.   [5] *Tufuna*.

such clear classification in Fiji? Either the Fijian system was earlier in the field, and the western Polynesian type is a later comer in which the four-caste system has already developed; or else the Fijian system is the same as the others but the fourfold classification has become obscure in accordance with the fluidity of Fijian culture, where everything is relative.

In favour of the first hypothesis there is the fact that the craftsmen in Fiji definitely belong to a later stratum.[1] In favour of the second there is the movement of the hill tribes down to the coast where they overwhelmed a Polynesian culture, adopting many of its features.[2]

I prefer to leave the matter *sub judice.*

[1] Above, p. 98.
[2] Hocart, "Early Fijians," *J.R.A.I.,* 1919, 42.

Rotuma

ROTUMA is a small island some 300 miles north of
Fiji. It has a peculiar language overlaid by at least
two Polynesian dialects.[1]

Rotuma interests us here for what it has not, rather than
for what it has. The kingship was reduced to a shadow.
It was represented by two puppets; the more shadowy of
the two is called the *Mu'a*, first, front, and the second and
more honoured is called *Sau*, like the Fijian king. Like
the Roman consuls, they were annual, but the Rotuman
year is of six months only.[2]

It follows that there is no royal family. That is perhaps
why the Rotumans never (to my knowledge) speak of
"noble youths," but only of "chiefly men."[3] The power is
in the hands of seven village headmen. It is somewhat as
in Ceylon, where the royalty and the priesthood had
vanished and left the farmer caste in possession. As in
Ceylon, the upper strata, the families of the ruling headmen, have become a new aristocracy, and enjoy the status
which the nobility enjoy elsewhere. The feudal services,
however, are much simplified. There are leaders of the
vanguard and there are lords of the green,[4] but they do
not haunt Big House, as in Fiji. I lived for some time
with the headmen, and there was no court.

There were wars which gave the stronger side the *mālō*,
victory, hegemony. The village headman who prevailed
appointed the kings. He also had the authority, *pure*

---

[1] Hocart, "Notes on Rotuman Grammar," *J.R.A.I.*, 1919, 252.

[2] There is a front year and a back year in every year.

[3] *Fā ñañaca* (sing).

[4] *Fū mara'e*.

the same word with the same meaning as the Tongan and the Samoan *pule*, to pray, to rule. Thus in Rotuma the attributes of noble and councillor are combined in one person. It is as if in India both *kshatra* and *brahma* were vested in one ruler.

Rome

FROM the Far East we jump to the West with seeming recklessness, but with some method; for Rome seems to have gone the same way as Rotuma and Ceylon; extinction of the royal and of the priestly caste, usurpation of the farmers.

Such at least seems to be the hypothesis that best explains the facts which we shall now detail.

To begin with, the archaic basis of society is ritual. Even in later times a man who was not included in the census was in the position of an outcaste, was stripped of his property and could be beaten and sold.[1] Now, this census was concluded by a solemn purification of the assembled people. The lustre, as this ceremony was called, was a kind of wholesale initiation. Full male citizenship and ritual participation went together: foreigners, prisoners and women were bidden by the lictor to depart before certain ceremonies.[2] All foreigners were not excommunicates. Aristocrats like Attus Clausus and the Tarquins could migrate into Rome with their retainers, assume aristocratic rank and enter the Senate, for they had their cult.[3]

Roman like Indian society was divided into sacrificial and non-sacrificial, patricians and plebeians. "Romulus, when he had marked off the better people from the inferior, next defined what each should engage in; the well-born, to sacrifice and rule, and judge, and with him administer the state, confining themselves to the affairs of the city; the plebeians to be released from these

[1] Dionysius of Halicarnassus, *Antiquitates*, IV, 15, 6.
[2] Festus, *s.v. exesto*.
[3] Livy, II, 16.

duties, neither having experience of them, nor on account of their poverty any leisure, and to cultivate and breed cattle and practice money-earning crafts.''[1] The aristocrats were "the good" or "the best.''[2]

Professor H. J. Rose thinks Johannes Lydus is not far wrong when he says all Roman magistrates were priests originally.[3] Some of them represent the royal powers put into commission, and the king was undoubtedly a ritual personage; so much so that the title passed under the republic to a sacrificer whose functions were purely ritual.[4] Another prerogative of his, the *imperium*, passed to other more secular magistrates, but it had evidently a ritual basis, for confederates who had refused to recognize the *imperium* of Rome admitted it once the temple of the confederation had been fixed in Rome.[5] In early Rome, as in Fiji, allegiance followed the temple.

Another aspect of the king's authority was even more obviously ritual. He took the omens. "Nothing could be done in war or peace unless after taking the auspices"; "nothing could be changed, no innovation made, unless the birds were favourable.''[6]

Where was the priestly caste? We have seen that in Fiji it is not as fully differentiated from other heads of houses as in India and Persia. Perhaps it was even less so in Rome; perhaps it once existed and became extinct as in Ceylon, or scarcely recognizable. I leave it to scholars to hunt for it.

There is no harm in making hypotheses; on the contrary, it is absolutely necessary to the progress of science. It seems to me legitimate, in view of the comparative evidence, to suggest that after the expulsion of the kings the power passed entirely into the hands of the

[1] Dion, Hal., II, 8.   [2] *Boni, optimates.*
[3] *The Roman Questions of Plutarch* (1924), 81.
[4] Cp. *Kings and Councillors*, 165.   [5] Livy, I, 45; cp. II, 38.   [6] *Ibid.*, I, 36.

third estate. This was known as the *patres*, fathers, heads of houses, a title which in India has become synonymous with the third or farmer caste.[1]

Every head of the family was a priest at the hearth. Every family had its hereditary cult; and the priests of Hercules, of the Sun, and other deities, were just the heads of families in which the cult was an heirloom.[2]

The plebs was not allowed to attend the sacred rites of the patricians, nor were they allowed to intermarry with them till 445 B.C.[3]

We have identified the plebs with the fourth caste of India, but there is another caste in Rome which can make as good a claim if not a better one. The patricians had their retainers, clients.[4] The patron had domestic jurisdiction over his clients, assigned to them fields they could cultivate, led them into battle, levied contributions in money; he had also duties to his clients, such as that in standing by them in lawsuits, and these rights were upheld by religion. How are we to decide between the plebs and the clients?

Much has been written about the plebs by specialists in Roman affairs without apparently arriving at any final conclusion. When the direct attack comes to a standstill, it is time for comparative evidence to try to turn the position. We note one result achieved by the experts. They tend to the conclusion that plebeians and clients had a common origin. The ancients declared that at the foundations of Rome the plebeians were distributed among the patricians as clients. That may only be their theory. Some moderns have reversed it and think that a germ of the plebs is the group of king's clients who stood

---

[1] Above, p. 59.

[2] Dion, Hal., II, 66.

[3] Pauly-Wissowa, *s.v. confarreatio*, 862; *clientes*, 43.

[4] *Clientes*, from *cluere*, to hear. They are those who obey.

K

in a direct relation to the State, and who lost their lord when the kings were driven out.[1] That might happen also to the retainers of patricians. Thus the twelve families of Potitii numbering thirty adults became totally extinct in one year. What became of their clients?

At this point the Tamils of North Ceylon come to our help. They divide the fourth caste into *kuḍimai* and *aḍimai*, household and external serfs.

The usual theory of conquest has been brought in to account for the Roman clients and plebeians, but the institution of client is much older than Rome, since it existed among the Sabines, the Etruscans and the Greeks.[2] That is indeed the invariable tale. No one has ever yet found a conquest which brought servitude or class differences into existence: they always were there already, and conquest has merely caused a reshuffle.

Heredity was evidently not a sufficient qualification for aristocratic rank. The young patrician had to undergo an initiation which consisted in the assumption of "the manly robe."[3]

As elsewhere, the king is the fount of power. Hence those legends according to which Romulus divided Rome into patricians and plebeians.[4] We have learnt how to interpret these legends: they do not record origins, but cases in which an existing custom was applied; they show us the king, not creating a social organisation, but confirming and adjusting it. We see Tarquin the Ancient exercising this prerogative when "he promoted one hundred persons to the Senate, who were afterwards called the minor clans."[5]

When Roman organization was transferred from a basis of birth to one of wealth, the prerogative continued; with the splitting up of the royal power it descended to

---

[1] Pauly-Wissowa, 24, 48.   [2] Livy, II, 16. Dion, Hal., IX, 5; II, 9.
[3] *Toga virilis.*   [4] Plutarch, *Romulus*, XIII.   [5] Livy, I, 35, 6.

the censors.[1] They could deprive a knight of his horse and expel from the Senate those who lived in a disorderly manner.[2] Two hostile censors once degraded each other, and one of them went so far as to degrade the whole people, except one tribe, to the lowest class.[3] That was mere folly, and the Senate had to intervene; but on another occasion the censors degraded 2,000 men with such good reason that the Senate supported them.[4] Offenders could be interdicted from fire and water, which was putting them out of communion, and a prisoner was not admitted to the rites.[5]

What little the ancients have preserved for us about early Roman society is sufficient to show that its general principles are the same as in India: division into sacrificial and non-sacrificial, initiation, degradation of the unfit, royal prerogative to raise or abase. Whether the resemblance went any further and the sacrificial class was originally divided into two or three we may leave to experts to debate. It is a secondary matter whether a priestly caste is differentiated between the royal and the landed, or remains embedded among the heads of houses.

[1] Livy, I, 42.　　[2] Plutarch, *Marcus Cato*, XVI.
[3] Livy, XXIX, 37, 8.　　[4] *Ibid.*, XXIV, 18, 7.　　[5] *Ibid.*, XXIV, 4.

Greece

IF we are asked whether Greek society was divided
into sacrificial and non-sacrificial, we shall certainly
answer no. Yet tucked away in the corners there are to
be found traces of such a division in historical times.
Aristotle is of opinion that "neither a peasant nor a craftsman should be appointed priest; for it is by the citizens
that the gods should be properly honoured." He ap-
proves of the Thessalian "free public square," not free in
the sense that it is open to all gratis, but, on the contrary,
because it is closed to the lower orders, free from their
debasing presence, "kept pure of all merchandise, and
which no craftsman or peasant or any such person is to
come near unless summoned by the magistrates." To
understand the significance of this exclusion, we must bear
in mind that this square is sacred.[1] The Greeks made
very much the same distinction as the Sinhalese between
the "best people" or the "fair and good," as opposed to
the bad, only they based it more on occupation, especially
on the distinction of liberal and manual occupations, than
on descent, a point of view which comes very near to ours.

We shall search Homer in vain for evidence of this
distinction between sacrificial and non-sacrificial, as we
shall search in vain for many other things, because he is a
narrator, not an expounder of custom. He does not pause
to tell us whether the serfs were excluded from the market-
place or not, because that is irrelevant to his story. We
have however evidence much older than Homer, if we are
not afraid of using myths as evidence of customs. We have
learned outside Greece how to interpret the myths of the

[1] Arist., *Pol.*, VII, 1,329 *a* 28 *ff.*, IV, 1,331 *a* 30 *ff.*

gods and giants, or the gods and titans: as reliable
traditions of recurrent ritual contests between impersonators of the light gods and of the dark gods, of those who
participate in the ritual of life, and those who represent
the powers of darkness and death. It may, of couse, be
that these myths were inherited from Mycenæan or
Minoan predecessors and represent a pre-Hellenic state
of society.

The have-nots are always revolting against the haves,
and as admission to the State cults is a distinct advantage,
conferring power, and so wealth, the non-sacrificial
classes are always trying to rise into the sacrificial ranks. In
Greece the revolt eventually became a struggle for admission to the magistracies and the franchise, to full
citizenship; but to the end this involved participation in
the cults, for the Greeks never divorced the State and the
ritual to the same extent as we have done.

Initiation survived into historical times. At the
festival of the Apatouria the boy was inducted into the
clan, and his admission was marked by the offering to
Zeus of a sheep or goat and of wine. Each member of the
clan received a share, just as in India eating with the
members is the essential part of admission or readmission.[1]

In Sparta birth was not sufficient and could even be
dispensed with. The son of a citizen had to qualify by
going through the necessary training, and retained his
citizenship by sending his quota to the mess. The first
condition corresponds to the martial exercises of the
Indian nobility; the second to the eating in common.
Those who were unable to contribute were classed as
inferiors. In early times a stranger who underwent the
discipline could become a Spartan.[2]

Purity was a condition of taking part in sacrifices or

[1] Pauly-Wissowa, *s.v. apatouria*. Gilbert, I, 185.
[2] Plutarch, *Inst. Lac.*, 21 *f.* Xenophon, *Respublica Lac.*, X, 7.

public functions. The two were bound up together, since every public function is accompanied by ritual. The ritually impure, such as murderers, are therefore excluded from both.[1] The sodomist is not allowed "to become one of the nine archons, to fill the office of priest, or to be a lawyer among the people or hold office . . . or be sent as a herald, or express his opinion, or attend the public sacrifices, or wear a wreath at the wreath-bearing festival, or enter the lustrated parts of the public squares."[2]

Homeric society, so far as we can gather from stray hints, was divided into nobles, commons and serfs. A threefold division still commended itself to Hippodamos of Miletus. He classified the citizens of his Utopia into arms-bearers, farmers and artisans.

The nobility was of royal descent. Even in historical times we are told that those were called nobles who inhabited the city and partook of the royal lineage.[3]

The title of king, *basileus*, seems to be applied by Homer to all the members of this aristocracy, like the title *turaña* in Fiji. This was the practice in Ephesus and Skepsis in historical times.[4] In Athens the "tribal kings" were those who superintended the tribal ritual, the equivalent more or less of the Fijian chieftains.[5] The title has thus had the same downward career as in Ceylon; and when Homer speaks of kings it is sometimes doubtful, as in Fiji, whether he means kings or nobles.

The kingship, as in Fiji, early Rome, and probably in early India, did not necessarily pass from father to son. Telemachus' grievance against the claimants to the throne left vacant by his father Odysseus is not that they

[1] Euripides, *Orestes*, 1594 *ff*.
[2] Æschines, *In Tim.*, 21.
[3] *Etym. Magnum*, *ap*. O. Schrader, *Reallexikon der indogermanischen Altertumskunde*, new ed. (Strassburg, 1927-8), *s.v. Stände*.
[4] Pauly-Wissowa, V, 66. Gilbert, II, 272. Strabo, XIV, 1, 3.
[5] *Phylobasileis*. Gilbert, I, 115.

are trying to usurp, but that they are eating up his patrimony.

The king is divine, godlike, cherished of Zeus, born of Zeus. He is from Zeus, whereas the bards are from Apollo.[1] Zeus is the thunder-god, conqueror of giants, dragon-slayer, and so the Greek equivalent of Indra. The king, however, is not as closely identified with the gods as his more eastern equivalents.

He is a ritual personage; he conducts the sacrifice, opens the ceremony with lustration, sprinkling of barley, and with prayer.[2] These are his most essential functions, for when the later Greeks split up the king's power among elected magistrates the title of king went to the one who had charge of the State sacrifices.

The Homeric kings spent much of their time in what looks like mere banqueting, but Homer calls it sacrificing.[3] They recall the Fijian kings receiving daily offerings of food, and sitting with their old men feasting, drinking, and talking. The sacrificial character of the royal meal has spread to every household, so that Plutarch considers every meal to be a religious ceremony, for, he says, "the table is something holy," and "it is by some called the hearth."[4]

In Crete and Sparta these common meals presided over by the king were daily and important in the warrior's life, like our officers' messes. Their ritual character appears in the fact that part of any animal sacrificed had to be sent to the mess.[5]

Being closely associated with the thunder god, the king and his caste were warlike, and they looked upon war as their special merit. This military character was developed to an extreme degree in Sparta and Crete. It was not that

[1] *Il.*, II, 188. Hesiod, *Theogony*, 95 *f.*   [2] *Od.*, III, 444 *f.*
[3] *Od.*, XIV, 27, etc.   [4] *Quæst. Rom.*, 64. *Symp.*, VII, 4, 7.
[5] Grote, *History of Greece*, II, 298.

they alone fought, but they held the same position in Greece as the feudal nobility of the Middle Ages, that of bearers of a very stringent tradition which imposed upon them a standard of military honour denied to the base crowd. Odysseus thus chides a man of the people: "Wretch, sit still and hear the words of others who are better than thou, while thou art unwarlike and feeble nor of any account in war and council."[1] Mechanical labour especially seemed inconsistent with excellence in war and council. This feeling persisted right through. The Greeks considered "those citizens who learned handicrafts and their descendants inferior, and thought those who were free from manual work to be noble, especially those addicted to war."[2] In Thebes the citizenship was granted to those who had abstained from manual occupations for some time.[3] The only occupations for a gentleman, a citizen as they would put it, were war and public affairs,[4] and the cult of the gods.[5] Even democracy did not break down the association between war and government: in Athens a period of military training preceded admission to the citizenship.[6]

I have pointed out elsewhere that Zeus has combined in himself the attributes, which are elsewhere kept apart, of the thunder-god and the sky or sun-god.[7] The first smites the evil ones, the other upholds law and order in the world. This theology reflects society: the Homeric king unites the functions of the two gods. Elsewhere there are two kings, one militant, the other judging. In Greece a single individual does both, though there are traces of a former duality. Sarpedon as king "protects Lycia by his judgments and his strength."[8] Aristotle

[1] *Il.*, II, 200. [2] Hdt., II, 167. [3] Arist., *Pol.*, VI, 1,329 *a* 28 *ff.*
[4] *Bouleutikon.* [5] Arist., *Pol.*, VII, 1,329 *a* 30 *ff.*
[6] Arist., *Athenaion Politeia*, 42, 3-5.
[7] *Kings and Councillors*, XII, especially 164; 282.
[8] *Il.*, XVI, 542. *Kingship*, 47.

describes the Homeric kings as "in possession of the military authority and of such sacrifices as were not in the hands of the priests, and in addition they decided legal cases."[1]

Staff-bearing is a common epithet of kings, yet it is not their exclusive attribute; it belongs also to priests, judges, and heralds.[2] It seems as elsewhere to be associated with speech, for when anyone stands up to speak in the assembly the herald places the staff in his hands.[3] But elsewhere it belongs to the caste in charge of speech, not to the nobility. It would seem as if the Homeric nobility had acquired the right of speech by borrowing the emblem of speech from the master of ritual. Such things do happen. We have seen that a few Samoan noblemen have acquired the right of making speeches;[4] and we know that on occasions the Indian king "sets aside his own weapons, and with the weapons of a priest, becoming a priest, approaches the sacrifice."[5]

Inevitably the master of ritual must decline if he allows his sphere to be encroached upon by the nobility. In Greece he has so declined that no one seems to have recognized him in the *kerux* or herald. It may indeed appear far-fetched to identify this herald with the Indian brahman; yet if we go into details we shall find it hard to resist that conclusion.

The Greek herald is under the patronage of Hermes, and even wears the attributes of that god.[6] To dress up like a god is to be identified with that god. The god of the brahman is Agni. I have demonstrated elsewhere that—

Hermes=Agni.[7]

[1] Arist., *Pol.*, III, 1,285 *a* 9 *ff.*
[2] *Il.*, II, 86; I, 15; VII, 277. *Od.*, II, 231.
[3] *Od.*, II, 37.   [4] Above, p. 121.   [5] *Ait. Br.*, VII, 19.
[6] H. B. Walters, *History of Ancient Pottery* (London, 1905), II, 198.
[7] *Kings and Councillors*, 19.

The presumption is that—

Kerux=Brahman.

This presumption is confirmed if we examine the duties and privileges of the Greek herald. He speaks the introductory prayer at an assembly before the host sets out. He carries a staff. He is the companion of his king. He is a messenger of Zeus and of kings. He is a peacemaker and can separate royal combatants, as do Fijian heralds. He is inviolable.[1] His part in the sacrifice, however, is much humbler than the brahman's. He brings the victim, helps to prepare it and pours water over the sacrificer's hands, but the king has the more important part.[2] The pouring of water must not be regarded as a mere menial duty; it is a rite which is still to be observed in Ceylon.[3]

Originally the Greek herald was hereditary, and he continued to be so in conservative Sparta,[4] but in democratic states he became a despised town-crier chosen for his powerful voice, and in receipt of wages. Thus we can observe in Greece how a hereditary office about the king changes into a salaried public appointment, how the qualification of divine descent gives place to the qualification of physical suitability. Here we have an excellent example of that process which we commonly call secularizing, without having any clear ideas of what it is.

The herald has so declined that he does not stand out as the king's rival. The contest is not, as in India and Samoa, between the king and the master of ritual, but between the nobility and the commons.

[1] Thucydides, VI, 32. Plutarch, *Dion.*, 13. *Od.*, X, 59; 102. *Il.*, XXIV, 178; I, 320 *f.*; VII, 272 *ff.* Pausanias, I, 36, 3; III, 37, 6. Hdt., VII, 133-6.

[2] *Il.*, III, 116 *ff.*; XVIII, 558. *Od.*, I, 146. Cp. *Kings and Councillors*, 190.

[3] The Skt. term *dakshiñodaka*, auspicious water, shows that it is not merely a removal of dirt.

[4] Hdt., VII, 134, 1.

The commons appear in Homer under the name of
demos. This word also describes the country as opposed
to the city where the king resides with his officers.[1] In
historical times it means a township or commune. The
Homeric nobles despised the people and apparently only
summoned them to the assemblies in the public square to
hear their opinions, as is done in Samoa.[2] The affairs of
the State seem to have been discussed by the king and his
elders sitting over their wine like the Fijian king and
his chieftains over *kava*.[3] Certainly in historical times we
find the sacred Council of Elders[4] forming a senate. In
Sparta "when the people were gathered together no one
else was allowed to express an opinion, but the commons
had power to decide on the motion proposed by the
elders and the kings."[5]

The lowest order of Homeric society was the serf.[6]
Homer introduces us to one of them, the swineherd
Eumæus. His condition is not without honour: he is
"famed" and his epithet is "divine."[7] He is treated with
respect by his lord, the king; he has the courage to retort
to a nobleman and does so with impunity; he takes upon
himself to slaughter one of his master's pigs to feast a
stranger.

Here we may be allowed to digress in order to point
out how handicapped are those who depend entirely on
books. Liddell and Scott approach Greek culture with the
prejudice of their own time and class, with the idea that
to be a serf is to be always downtrodden. They cannot
conceive of his being called famous, so in their dictionary
they translate "notorious." We who have seen the
caste system at work know that a serf receives honour,
because he is a kind of priest and sometimes represents

---

[1] *Od.*, XI, 14. [2] *Il.*, II, 198; 48 *ff*. *Od.*, II, 1 *ff*.
[3] *Il.*, IV, 259: IV, 344 *ff*.; IX, 90. *Od.*, XIII, 8. [4] *Gerousia*.
[5] Plutarch, *Lykurgus*, 6. [6] *Thes.* [7] *Od.*, XVII, 385; XVI, 1.

gods.[1] We know that the record of that system is not one of
unmitigated oppression, but on the contrary it can be far
less oppressive than our industrial system. Its machinery
works far more smoothly because it is amply supplied with
the oil of etiquette. The lowest owe service which in
theory they cannot refuse, but no one can compel them
to render it with a will; they can only be heartened to it
by giving them whatever honour is their due, by always
addressing them by the title they bear, by "pleases"
and "be good enoughs," and even by terms of relationship
such as "my son," "O uncle." Their privileges have to
be respected, and at the same time prevented from extend-
ing unduly. Heredity, so far from placing them at the
mercy of their master, puts him in their hands; for you
can dismiss a hireling, but not a hereditary servant, and
so if you want to reap peace and good service you must
sow tact and good manners. Hereditary service is quite
inconsistent with the ruthless industrialism of our times,
and that is no doubt why it is painted in such black
colours. Give a dog a bad name. If we want to know the
truth, we must go and see. Not all can do so, and then the
next best is to read our *Odyssey*. Such a narrative has the
disadvantage of telling us little about social organization,
but the advantage of not being biased by party feeling.

Sparta preserved serfdom in what appeared to the
Athenians to be a very harsh form; but such opinions are
worth about as much as the views of our liberals about
Indian caste and African slavery.

Besides serfs, we hear of captives.[2] They may serve in
the house or in the fields.[3]

There appear in Homer's pages a number of specialists
or "public workers."[4] Their status is not clear, whether
they belong to the commons or the serfs. Some were
presumably serfs, for Aristotle tells us that "in ancient

[1] Above, p. 60.   [2] *Dmōes.*   [3] *Od.*, XIV, 3*f.*; XI, 489.   [4] *Dēmiourgos.*

times in some states the mechanic population consisted of slaves and foreigners; wherefore the great part are so now."[1] It may be there was no rule applicable to all states: we have seen that the status of carpenters varies in Fiji. Anyhow, these public workers include the heralds, soothsayers and bards, so they are not necessarily craftsmen. Bards, for instance, do not sing merely for pleasure, but sing dirges at funerals; they too are divine, from Apollo, and they are inspired by the Muse.[2] They hold then a kind of priesthood. Physicians, too, were governed by a god, Asklepios, and the art was once hereditary among the descendants of that god, descendants perhaps only through the ritual. Another public worker, the carpenter, is inspired by Pallas Athene.[3]

All such statements were imitated by our poets as pleasing fictions, and so we have got into the habit of thinking of them as no more than poetic ornament. We know, however, that there are still countries where washermen, poets, weavers, potters and all technicians owe their skill and success to the divine aid which is present in the instruments of their crafts.[4]

The smith is presumably also a public worker. He appears at the sacrifice to gild the victim's horns.[5] We hear of tumblers who perform to the music of the bards.[6]

These occupations must originally have been hereditary, for they were so in historical Sparta. Herodotos says: "The Lacedemonians resemble the Egyptians in this also: their heralds and flute-players and cooks inherit

[1] *Pol.*, III, 5 1,278 *a* 6 *ff.*

[2] *Od.*, XVII, 384; XIX, 135. *Il.*, XXIV, 721.

[3] *Il.*, XV, 412; V, 61.

[4] Above, p. 16.

[5] *Od.*, VIII, 73. This is still done at Egyptian festivals, but purely as a way of advertising an animal for slaughter. An interesting example of a ritual procedure being turned to commercial use.

[6] *Il.*, XVIII, 605.

the ancestral craft, a flute-player is born of a flute-player, a cook of a cook, a herald of a herald."[1]

I am not acquainted with any myth concerning the origin of the Greek classes, but the habit of ascribing all institutions to some king persisted to the end. Transmitted to our modern theorists, it has had disastrous effects on the study of the growth of social organization, as disastrous as the doctrine of special creation once had on biology.

In Crete it was Minos who had organized the State, in Athens Theseus, in Italy Italus.[2] The reason for these traditions is that the king was the expounder of right.[3] Later, when the monarchy was put in commission, the duty of laying down the law, or watching over rights, was entrusted to special officials.[4] In important crises one man was appointed to overhaul the whole State in the manner kings were fabled to have done. Such men are often credited with instituting what we know to be thousands of years older than their time. Thus Lykurgus is said to have "ordained that the king should perform all the public sacrifices on behalf of the city as being from the god."[5] We know that this duty is as old as kingship, which was already old 3,000 years B.C. This is the kind of error into which our specialists who stick to one area constantly fall. A little comparative study soon dispels it.

Some Greek cities still show seniority sorting out the citizens into classes. Aristotle says that "in some places a father and a son may not take part in the government, in some places the elder and the younger brother."[6] He points out that this has been the cause of many

---

[1] Hdt., VI, 60.

[2] Arist., *Pol.*, VII, 1,329 *b* 4 *ff.*

[3] *Dikē*=Skt. *dharma. Kingship*, 47 *ff.*

[4] *Thesmothetēs, thesmophylax, dikaskopos.* Gilbert, II, 165.

[5] Xenophon, *Reip. Lac*, XV, 2.

[6] Just as, in Tonga, only the head of the family sits in the ring.

revolutions, "kinsmen falling out among themselves, because few only had a share in the government." Thus in Marseilles, Istros and Heracleia "those who had no share in the offices agitated until they were admitted, first the elder sons and later the younger."[1]

Here Aristotle touches upon one of the main causes of revolutions, a social exclusiveness which corresponds to no differences in natural endowments, since those inside may be of the same breed as those without. If the outside pressure becomes too great there is an explosion.

[1] Arist., *Pol.*, V, 1,305 *a* 4 *ff.*

Egypt

IN Egypt we return from the scrappiness of texts to the fullness of life. We can ask about anything we like, instead of depending on what chance has saved from the wreckage, and we can always check the accuracy of our own or other people's observation.[1]

In our inquiries we very soon discover that Egypt has lost the last vestiges of feudalism, and has travelled far on the road to secularization and nationalization.

Let us take the barber as an example. His ceremonial character has dwindled away and the last vestiges are now disappearing. One of his most important duties is to circumcise; that is part of the religion, but his role in this ceremony is now reduced to that of a technician, a surgeon. He used to walk in the procession, as Sinhalese barbers do at a wedding; but now seldom does so. I have met a man near Cairo who used to do so until a few years ago. The Government licenses him for minor operations. This has no doubt contributed a good deal to turn him into a surgeon pure and simple; for to be an official is to be somebody, and so he lays great stress on his official capacity. Now the Government's point of view in these matters is purely secular.

What exactly do we mean by "secular"? We have been using the word, and it is time we made clear to ourselves exactly what we mean by secular as opposed to ritual. We can do so best by examining concrete examples.

The Fijian barber is purely ritual—in fact, he can only be called "barber'" by stretching words; for the reason of

[1] I have drawn largely on 'Ali Ahmed 'Isa Effendi's thesis on the organization of a village in the Delta.

his existence is to play his part in an organization which is based on a belief that life and death are entities that pass from one to another according to our wishes, if we possess the secret of controlling them; against our wishes if we do not. To put ourselves into this point of view we should go back to the time when we did not know of microbes. We then thought of smallpox, cholera, and other such epidemics as things which passed from one person to another. Or rather we did not think, but we spoke and acted as if we thought so. In the same way, many peoples on earth talk and act as if life and death were infections capable of being controlled, even though they may have no definite ideas on the subject. In the same way most Englishmen talk and act as if communism were a virus that travelled about, though they would repudiate the idea if put to them as clearly as that. Whatever the Fijian barber may think he certainly acts as if something passed from the king's body on to his hands, something that could be rubbed off on a stone, and with that stone thrown away.

The Egyptian barber's work, on the other hand, has quite another basis. He has given up all attempts at infusing life, energy, success, or at drawing out death, sickness, weakness, failure (unless he still preserves some charms unofficially). His technique is now based on contact, on the fact that one thing displaces another. He has nothing to do with the spiritual value of circumcision, with its place in a scheme to bring a boy to a successful manhood;[1] his part is merely to remove a bit of skin by the pressure of a sharp edge. He does not help to make a marriage fruitful and the village prosperous by removing anything adverse to life, anything polluting; he just beautifies the bridegroom by mechanical means. He has become just an expert, one who has nothing to do with

[1] Hocart, "Initiation and Manhood," *Man*, 1935, 23

L

the direction of life, but is merely commissioned to carry out a mechanical process. True, after his operations he keeps sickness and death away with his antiseptics, but their use is based on a physical theory and not on a theory of disease as a thing that flies about. What he thinks about them I do not know, and it does not much matter for our present purpose. The reason why he uses them is not that he understands them, but that in Europe there is a belief that they have a physical action on certain organisms that attack any flesh with which they can come into contact. This conviction is accepted in medical circles in Egypt and by them the technique is imposed on the barber.

It is, however, only by tracing the barbership to its ritual origins that we can explain the strange medley of his duties: circumcision, cupping, shaving, beautifying the bridegroom, etc. There is no technical convenience in combining these activities, and when they receive a mechanical basis they tend to fall apart as they have done in Europe.

Let us now consider the barber from the point of view of what I have, for want of a better term, called national-ization.[1] The village barber is not a retainer, but a functionary; he does not work for a lord, but for the villagers, and he does not look upon them as a collective manorial lord, as in Ceylon. The Lower Egyptian barber is not a servant, but a craftsman who exchanges his expert skill for food. He does not hold land, but has a kind of retaining fee from all who employ him, a fee which takes the shape of so many measures of wheat and maize twice a year. It may seem a small difference whether

[1] I do not want to suggest that there is any connection between the process I am here describing and what our politicians call nationalization. It may be that this latter is merely a continuation of the former, but until that is proved it is certainly confusing to use the same word for what may be different phenomena, and I should welcome a better word.

he holds land and gets the produce out of it himself, or whether he receives the produce of the land through others; yet it is a big difference, for it makes him into a more extreme specialist, since he no longer cultivates. It also gives him a freer market, and so loosens the personal relationship.

Of the other village specialists some are still purely ritual. The washerman of the dead is a peasant who washes, dresses, admonishes the deceased, and sees him to his grave. He still retains the word of power which is so important an attribute of priesthood, and which still prevents us from regarding him as a pure craftsman. The *fiqih* or teacher is dedicated entirely to the word, by which he prepares people for the good life which emanates from the scriptures, and even (*sub rosa*) from charms. The masters of the word resist secularization longest, but it is doubtful if they ever completely succeed. In our country they are trying hard; they repudiate the old ideas of a transferable life contained in forms and words, only to substitute other entities such as culture, civilization, liberty, communism, etc., of which they speak as if they were invisible substances spreading like gas. The subject of their discourse is different, but the mental process is the same. In fact it is hard to see how dealers in words can ever be secularized in the sense in which we are here using the word, since they work with ideas, and not with their hands, and so they cannot become mechanized, unless they are mere reciters of other people's words like gramophones. Of these there are many in Egypt to be seen at every fair.

There are other specialists who can no longer be called functionaries. They are craftsmen pure and simple, that is their work is reduced almost entirely to skilful manipulation, and no longer includes the infusion of luck or some such entity into their work. It may be that a few charms survive; but there is no definite theology such as exists among the Indian craftsmen, no belief that the deity is present in their material or their tools. Their religion forbids that. One potter will not even put religious texts on his pots, because he does not think it good to burn the name of God. Unlike the barber, the potter does not receive a retaining fee, but sells each piece. He lives in or near the village because he has to live somewhere, but he is not attached to the village. He sends his goods all over the country and into the town. If each village were a nation we should say he was international.

Thus in Egypt we can observe different stages of secularization and nationalization, and we note that it is those occupations which can be narrowed down most to manual action that advance quickest in that direction.

The status of the peasant in Lower Egypt is much lower than further east. This may be due to oppression and overcrowding. Escape from a hard lot is sought in occupations which in India would be below the peasant's dignity. I know of one peasant who has taken to barbering in order to escape the hard life of a cultivator. Besides, he is almost a government official. It is different in parts of Syria. In Homs and Hama, for instance, the peasants look down on the craftsmen and refuse to intermarry with them, just as in India.[1] There are traces of such an attitude in Egypt. I was admonished not to address the car-washer by the title of his occupation, but by his name, because he cleaned machines; but cooking is a good occupation, so you say, "O cook."

Terms of relationship are usual, but since caste has ceased to exist they have no connection with caste.

In conclusion, Egypt has evolved much more as regards social organization than any of the people we have

[1] Kazem Daghestani, Etude Sociologique sur la famille musulmane en Syrie. Paris (1932).

reviewed. Yet we are constantly told that the peasants of Egypt are primitive, most primitive. If by primitive we mean poor, and so unable to keep up an elaborate style of living, then they are primitive indeed. But if we mean what the word originally meant, that it is near to the parent form, then the social organization of the Egyptian peasant is the reverse of primitive. It has evolved further than that of our forefathers up to about the Renaissance.

Origins and Tendencies

THE comparative philologists once made it their ambition to reconstitute vanished languages, even to the extent of writing in the hypothetical Aryan. They have now given up that ambition, and we should be wise to follow their example. Whether such a reconstitution is possible or not, it is not worth while. When we have reconstituted a lost language or social organization, what have we gained? Nothing but a picture, unless it explains later developments; but if all we want is to explain why not concentrate on that and leave out the reconstituting?

In the present case our aim is not to describe the social organization that flourished in such and such a place at such and such a time before our records begin, but to explain the characteristics of living societies, and this we can do without reconstituting any particular society. We may never know how Palæolithic man was organized, and I do not for my part care if we don't; but we can say that the caste systems of India, Persia, Fiji, Samoa, and Tonga, and even the casteless system of modern Egypt is best explained as growing out of a society of which the main principles are perhaps best preserved in Fiji, though some are perhaps better preserved elsewhere. It is a society headed by a king who is responsible for the life of the people and of the things on which the life of the people depends: crops, cattle, fish, sunshine, the world. In this task he requires the assistance of various chieftains who are in charge of the various departments. Why this should be, or why the duties should be divided in the way they are it is not possible to explain on the present evidence. In particular cases we can sometimes just see where the explanation lies. The barber is originally the man who touches the king's body. When his original character has been obscured, and his duties come to be based on manual skill and social convenience, these duties are readjusted. Fortunately for the theorist, there is always a lag in the readjustment; the old custom survives for some time after the point of view that gave rise to it has vanished. Thus in Egypt hairdressing and minor surgery continue to be associated after the reason for this association has disappeared, much to the advantage to the student of social evolution.

When we have found a formula to explain the barber's duties, we find ourselves face to face with a further problem: why should there be only one man who can touch the king's body? Here we can try two hypotheses: either he is the only man who can do so without being blasted by the king's supernatural power, or else one man is selected to endure the ensuing disabilities, such as not being able to handle his food, because it would obviously be highly inconvenient if everyone were liable to be hampered in this way. Supposing further research decides in favour of the first hypothesis, then we shall be asked to explain why that particular man is safe in touching the king's body. Is it due to the degree of kinship between his ancestors and the king? And so on and so on; for in science every solution raises a new problem and there is no end.

Thus in time we must accumulate an increasing number of formulæ, but we have to see that they are not mutually contradictory. We cannot, for instance, explain the combination of pot-making and bone-setting in India by the creative functions of the potter, and elsewhere put it down to the confluence of separate activities. We must be consistent, and when we find contradictions we

must revise our formulæ so as to bring them into harmony
with one another, and so explain the largest possible number
of facts with the smallest possible number of hypotheses.
That eventuality, however, is a long way off. We are only
just beginning to trace large numbers of social facts to
common roots. We might be further advanced if we had
not wasted so much time in trying to reconstitute the
exact image of primitive man.

When we have traced a number of social phenomena
to their roots, we shall notice that certain processes
keep recurring. We have noted especially two which
we have provisionally called secularization and nationalization.

Secularization is not one long line of development
from prehistoric times down to the present, as one would
imagine from most works on the evolution of culture,
but one that is constantly taking place. It consists, as
we have seen, in the narrowing down of a wide, embracing
pattern of behaviour to a limited range of mechanical
actions. Thus a priest has to shape clay in the course of
the ritual to represent the things into which life is to be
infused; then this priest limits his activities to the shaping
of clay, but it remains for him a process which is not
purely mechanical, for the god is present in a lump
of clay, and on him depends success. That is the stage
reached in India. Then he drops everything but mechanical
processes; he becomes a mechanic pure and simple,
relying for success merely on his eye and hand, and
knowledge of physical conditions favourable to the
making of good pots.

This is a process that keeps occurring again and again,
and we may say there is a tendency always in that direction. Is it only a tendency, or is it an inevitable development? It is generally assumed that the process can be
reversed. In fact, all theories of primitive culture have

been based on the assumption that primitive man was secularly minded, a pure craftsman, free from all this putting of life into things; then magic crept into his works and tainted them with nonsense, and now we are busy once more reversing the process. Unfortunately, no effort has ever been made to prove that a purely secular activity can be desecularized. Until actual cases are produced, until we find a carpenter, for instance, giving up pure mechanics for a belief in the divinity of his tools, we cannot take seriously a theory which is based on the assumption that such things happen.

Secularization is merely a form of specialization; it involves a narrowing down of the attention and interest. The problem of desecularization is therefore bound up with another: is despecialization possible? The people of Levuka in Lakemba seem to answer the question in the affirmative. It is said that formerly they did not plant, but navigated and fished only; now they cannot be distinguished as to their activities from the other Lakembans, who are as unspecialized as they can be. The whole problem, however, is too big to be decided on such meagre evidence. We are safer in observing what goes on round about us.

It is possible that nationalization and specialization—consequently, secularization—are connected. The more highly specialized a man is the more he approximates to a machine, and so the less weight he bears in the general affairs of life. The court of the king or lord in a feudal society requires men who have a grasp of affairs. The specialists have improved their achievement in one line, but have diminished their usefulness in the wider spheres of life. Our village blacksmith is not an ornament to the manor; the Tongan carpenter graces his Fijian chief's *kava* ring, because he is more of a councillor than a craftsman. On the other hand, our village blacksmith commands a respect which the highly specialized factory worker does not inspire.

Specialization does not improve the status, but tends to exclude from the inner circle. The possession of manual skill tempts to specialization. We can see the beginnings of this in Fiji. The Tongan carpenter is attached to the king as chieftain, but it is not as chieftain that his services are sought by others, but as craftsman. Thus emphasis is laid on his craftsmanship to the detriment of his councillorship. We can see the consequences beginning to appear: I was present once when he sat on the right of his chief where he would have had to direct the ceremonial; but he did not know all the words so he had to change places with the acting councillor on the left who was not a craftsman and did know.[1] In India the carpenter still comes fairly high, next to the farmers, precisely because he is less mechanized than ours.

In our Lakemban example nationalization and specialization go hand in hand. The carpenter is tending to specialize because he has a speciality which is wanted by others besides the king. Nationalization, however, is to some extent independent of specialization. The Indian barber and washerman are pretty well nationalized; everyone who is of good standing makes use of their services; in the Kandyan country that means the big majority of the people. They want specialists, however, not because shaving and washing are difficult manual operations best done by one who devotes his whole time to them, but for reasons of purity. It is impossible to explain the early appearance of the barber or washerman on technical grounds. Anyone can cut hair, and in Fiji everyone does so, except for a person of much higher rank. Washing is easy, especially in countries that dress with one piece of cotton and have plenty of clean streams

[1] *Lau*, 62.

with big stones. Given space and servants, it is easy
enough in our own overdressed society, and some of us
can recall the days when the washing was done at home
and hung on the line in the garden. The reason why
specialists are needed for tasks which could be quite well
done by the household has been hinted at in Ceylon: it
lies in ideas about birth, menstruation, and death. The
spread of these functionaries throughout all classes is not
due to technical difficulty, but to a very common motive,
snobbery. Everyone likes to imitate his betters, the big
feudal nobles the king, the small nobles the big ones, and
so on down to the lowest stratum. It is a process that we
can observe about us every day. It has been traced over
long periods in Egypt, with the surprising result that we
owe our souls and immortality to the imitation of royal
style.[1] Thus royal ways filter down to the common people,
sometimes slowly, sometimes with astonishing rapidity,
but naturally shorn of their pomp. The poor peasant can
only produce a very simplified copy of the royal state,
and often a collective copy only. His resources do not
suffice to maintain his own barber, carpenter, fisherman,
as do those of a king or great nobleman. He must share,
but a barber who is shared by many soon loses his
character of service tenant and becomes a free craftsman.
Thus the apparent degradation of the royal style becomes
a step in social evolution. For good or for evil, the crafts
are freed from their feudal setting and can be isolated and
concentrated upon, so that greater skill results, also a
greater freedom of markets. A more highly differentiated
society arises with all the advantages and disadvantages of
differentiation. Where there is much specialism greater

[1] G. A. Reisner, *The Egyptian Conception of Immortality*, London,
1912. A. Moret, *Le Nil et la civilization égyptienne*, Paris, 1926; trsl.
M. R. Dobie, London, 1927. Hocart, "Snobbery" in *Custom is King*, ed.
L. H. Dudley Buxton, London, 1937. Hocart, "Vulgarization," *Man*,
1937.

co-ordination is needed. As long as the co-ordination is adequate a highly differentiated society will prevail over a less highly differentiated, but if the co-ordination should fail to keep pace with the increasing specialism the state of that society is not to be envied by any feudal organization.

Index

Printed in Great Britain by
The Camelot Press Ltd., London and Southampton

CASTE